MW00475938

Illumination for Modern Calligraphers

Documents du Moyen-Age XVème siècle.

6_Des Heures illuminées (Naf. 1175 Bibl. Nat.)

7_Du Manuscrit (Franc. 20,072 Bibl. Nat)

1_Bordure d'un Manuscrit (Franc. 2678 Bibl. Nat.)

1.2.3.4.5. Tirés des Bordures du manuscrit (Franc. N° 54 Bibl. Nat).

Illumination for Modern Calligraphers

PRACTICAL IDEAS FROM NINETEENTH-CENTURY HANDBOOKS

Christopher Jarman

Watson-Guptill Publications/New York

Frontispiece and title pages.
Details of floral borders copied from French fifteenth-century manuscripts and Books of Hours. These details were painstakingly redrawn by Ernest Guillot for his book L'Ornamentation, *published in Paris in the 1890s, from which most of the illustrations in this book have been selected.*

This edition, design and Guillot illustrations Copyright © 1988 by Savitri Books Ltd
Text and line drawings Copyright © 1988 by Christopher Jarman

First published 1988 in New York by Watson-Guptill Publications
a division of Billboard Publications, Inc.
1515 Broadway, New York, N.Y. 10036

Library of Congress Cataloging-in-Publication Data

Jarman, Christopher.
    Illumination for modern calligraphers.

    Bibliography: p.
    Includes index.
    1. Illumination of books and manuscripts—Technique.
I. Title.
ND3310.J37 1988   745.6'7'028   87-34630
ISBN 0-8230-2534-9

All rights reserved. No part of this publication may be reproduced or used in any form or by any means—graphic, electronic, or mechanical, including photocopying, recording, taping, or information storage and retrieval systems—without prior written permission of the publisher.

Manufactured in Spain

First Printing, 1988

1 2 3 4 5 6 7 8 9/94 93 92 91 90 89 88

Pictures on pp. 6, 15, 22, 98, 99, 102, 103, 122 and 127 appear by courtesy of the Board of Trustees of the Victoria and Albert Museum.

Produced and designed by
Savitri Books Ltd
71 Great Russell Street
London WC1B 3BN
Managing editor and art direction: Mrinalini Srivastava

ACKNOWLEDGEMENTS

Grateful thanks are due to the many people who have helped me in compiling this book. For permission to draw upon their written works I am most grateful to Michael Gullick, Donald Jackson, Marie Angel, Sam Somerville and Mrs. A. S. Osley on behalf of the late Dr. Osley. Special thanks are due to Ethna Gallacher for her contribution to the practical projects contained in this book and for her sketches.

I am also particularly grateful for help and advice always generously given by Sue Cavendish, Hon. Secretary of the Society of Scribes and Illuminators.

Christopher Jarman, 1987

Savitri Books would also like to thank Miss Janet Backhouse, Assistant Keeper at the Department of Manuscripts in the British Library, Dr. Rowan Watson, Assistant Keeper (Special Collections) at the Victoria and Albert Museum Library and the library staff for their advice and practical help.

CONTENTS

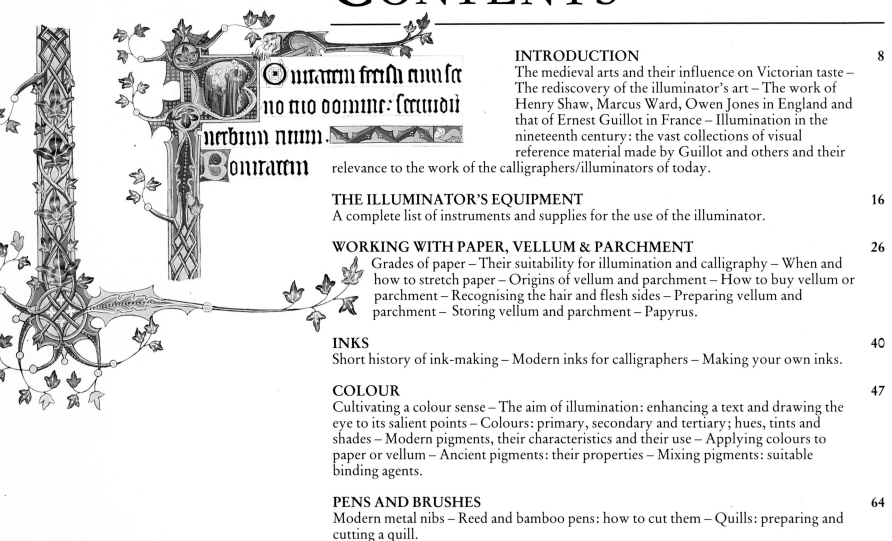

Left. *Border and initials copied by Henry Shaw and reproduced in his book:* Illuminated Ornaments from Manuscripts of the Middle Ages, *published in London in 1833. Henry Shaw was one of the pioneers who initiated research in the medieval arts and the working methods of the ancient scribes. The illuminated details reproduced in his book were drawn and engraved by him with immense care. But like other nineteenth-century illuminators, he could not emulate the calligraphic quality of the old scribes. The black text, which he probably wrote using a brush, looks decidedly crude next to the lovingly painted and illuminated borders and initials. Nevertheless, his book is one of the best of the many collections of ornamental details published in the nineteenth century and is a fine example of early chromolithographic printing.*

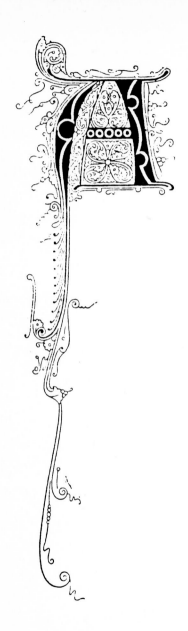

INTRODUCTION

It is only in the last quarter of the twentieth century that the virtues of Victorian taste, craftsmanship and design have been gradually rediscovered. Indeed, in the 1960s the word "Victorian" was used as a term of abuse. Whether it referred to moral values, household furniture or architecture, Victorian always implied stuffy, over-decorated, derivative, and just plain old-fashioned.

During the 1970s and 80s, however, the growth of nostalgia for the past and an intuitive reaction against a too-rapid computerization in design created a new interest in the nineteenth century, its artists and craftsmen. We wonder again at the astonishing accomplishments of such engineers as Brunel, designers like William Morris and many unknown builders and carpenters who spread Victorian style across the world in railroads, cities, art, everyday furnishings and domestic objects. The civic buildings of India and colonial Africa and the countless nineteenth-century inventions are now appreciated much more than they were even a decade ago. Much of the design in the arts, crafts and architecture of the Victorian Age, however, was inspired by the mood of the Middle Ages – which to the Victorians was mysterious, romantic, idyllic. The Gothic Revival Movement, which began in the late eighteenth century and was fuelled by the works of Sir Walter Scott, Shelley and Keats, gained impetus in the Victorian Age with the ballads and epic poems of Swinburne and Tennyson; all fostered this fascination with medieval ideas and artefacts, as well as the enormous amateur interest in archaeology. In addition, contemporary archaeological discoveries in Egypt were stimulating an equally romantic fascination with the images of the Pharaohs and the contents of the Pyramids.

Among the loveliest of all medieval items were the illuminated manuscripts, missals and books of hours of the tenth to the fourteenth centuries. Like the magic spells of Merlin or the mysteries of the Pyramids, the lost skills of making and colouring these gorgeous objects fascinated Victorian artists.

From the 1830s onwards, Henry Shaw, a talented illuminator, studied the collection of illuminated manuscripts in the British Museum and made copies of them. He was supported and aided by Sir Frederic Madden, who was then the Keeper of Manuscripts at the Museum. Madden wrote the excellent introduction to Henry Shaw's seminal book, *Illuminated Ornaments from Manuscripts of the Middle Ages*, which was published by William Pickering in 1833. Shaw was a talented illuminator. His copies of medieval manuscripts are painstakingly accurate with their engraved colour plates – the gold and all illustrative details finely reproduced. He was, however, a poor calligrapher and appears to have thought, like other Victorian artists, that the medieval scribes either used fine brushes or drew small black letters with a pointed quill. The copying of scribes' lettering was always of a low standard right up until the more serious studies of William Morris in the 1890s and somewhat mars the effect of the splendid illuminated work. But it was really through the genius of Edward Johnston that the old secrets of calligraphy were rediscovered. His book, *Writing & Illuminating, & Lettering*, which was first published in 1906, remains a classic.

The purpose of Shaw's book, however, was to provide material in a kind of catalogue of ideas for ornamentation, which could be used by illuminators, architects, artists and craftsmen. Marcus Ward, illuminator to Queen Victoria, and Vere Foster, an eminent Victorian philanthropist and writing master, evidently copied from Shaw's designs. Owen Jones, the art decorator who was superintendent of works for the London Exhibition of 1851 and director of decoration for the Crystal Palace, was similarly fascinated by medieval crafts and illumination in particular. His great work, the *Grammar of Ornaments*, originally published in 1856, remains the bible of Victorian aesthetics and has recently been reissued in the United Kingdom and in the United States.

As the nineteenth century progressed, the revival of archaeological and scholarly interest in illumination influenced a whole generation of artists, many of whom took up the craft so that a recognizable nineteenth-century style of illumination evolved.

Gradually, this serious interest in the subject filtered through to the public, and illumination became a highly popular hobby. This created a huge demand for suitable manuals and literature designed to teach calligraphy and decorated and illuminated

Left. *Black outline for a style of initials very commonly found in thirteenth-century manuscripts. The body of the letter would look attractive in a solid colour – using gouache – or gilded. The feathery tendrils should be done with a pen. Red or blue were colours frequently used for that purpose.*

9

letters, both at basic and at more advanced levels. Consequently, a plethora of books appeared. Many of these nineteenth-century manuals gave page after page of pre-drawn, intricately decorated letters along with a colour plate that acted as a model for the reader to follow and appropriately colour the letters. In this field, as in embroidery and other areas of the decorative arts, the Victorians displayed their love of rich colours.

Much of this "do-it-yourself" illumination is dated now, but in addition to these publications, aimed at "fair, young, idle hands," appeared real gems, books that reproduced painstakingly collected and copied elements of illumination and decorated letters.

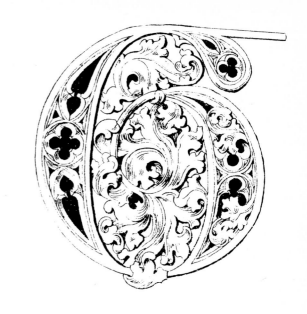

This book, which is aimed at modern calligraphers who wish to progress to illumination and decoration, is largely based on Ernest Guillot's *L'Ornementation* which was published in Paris *c*1890. Guillot assembled an extraordinary collection of alphabets, borders and motifs stretching from the Carolingian period in the eighth century to the eighteenth century. The initial letters, complete alphabets, motifs, borders and miniatures were all faithfully redrawn from a great variety of manuscripts as well as from such ornamental sources as architecture and furniture design.

This kind of publication became highly popular during the nineteenth century throughout Europe, but particularly in France and England. The great strides made by chromolithographic printing, which enabled subtle colours to be beautifully reproduced, contributed to making Guillot's book, and others of the same ilk, highly attractive objects that are now keenly sought by book collectors.

Guillot's book had no text, barring the small captions that are part of the plates and which state his sources. The purpose of his book was to catalogue ideas and visual

A typical example of pre-drawn ornamented initials from a calligraphy and illumination instruction manual published in England in the 1890s. The left-hand page shows the final coloured and gilded result. The manual also gave pre-drawn outlines, as shown on this page, for readers to copy and illuminate. The letters were copied from an illuminated missal made in the fifteenth century in Nuremberg, but they have acquired an unmistakable Victorian Gothic feel, very reminiscent of the work of Owen Jones.

12

references to be used by illuminators and indeed by anyone interested in ornament in any sphere of the decorative arts.

Few copies of *L'Ornementation* have survived, but the chance discovery of one copy, in mint condition, gave birth to this book. It offers modern calligraphers and illuminators a unique and varied selection of material to be copied and amalgamated in pieces of traditional work, or to inspire them to adapt pieces more in keeping with today's less lavish taste. To begin to assemble such an exciting collection of alphabets, elaborate initials, richly decorated borders and motifs would be so time-consuming as to be an almost impossible task.

Throughout my text, I have assumed the reader to have a knowledge of calligraphy. For those who would like to learn more about it, I have pointed out a few useful books in the reading list. Similarly, a knowledge of drawing and painting is an asset to the would-be illuminator, but do not be discouraged if you are timid about drawing freehand. There is an enormous amount you can do simply by tracing from this book. Alternatively, you could restrict yourself to designs based on geometric patterns and simple, repeated motifs. The medieval artists' most stunning works are frequently based on very simple designs and their artistry relied heavily on

their deep knowledge of colours, the ways in which colours react to one another, and the patience and care they lavished on gilding, outlining and finishing their designs.

The calligrapher who has never before attempted to illuminate his or her work may be well advised to read the complete text of this book first, to look at the illustrations in detail, to become familiar with the sections that should be referred to later and then to experiment with a small and simple piece of work. Some of the ingredients used in gilding, for instance, may sound like alchemy. But with a little practice and dedication, you will soon find that very attractive pieces can be produced, even by a novice. The golden rule in illumination is not to attempt too much at first. Far more real progress is made by carefully, patiently and accurately completing a single copy of one simple letter than in hurrying over half a dozen more ambitious projects.

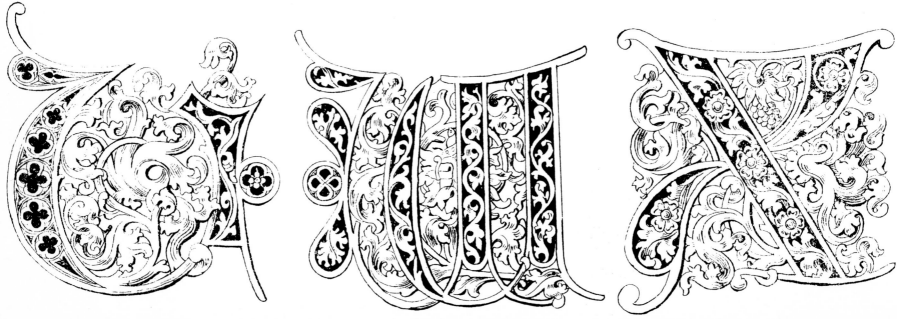

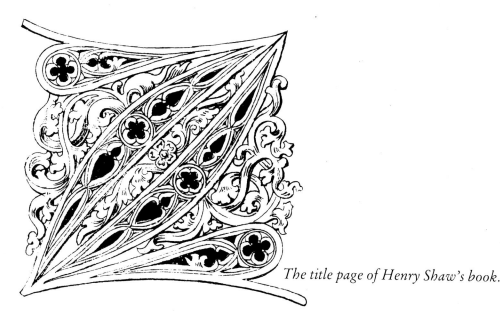

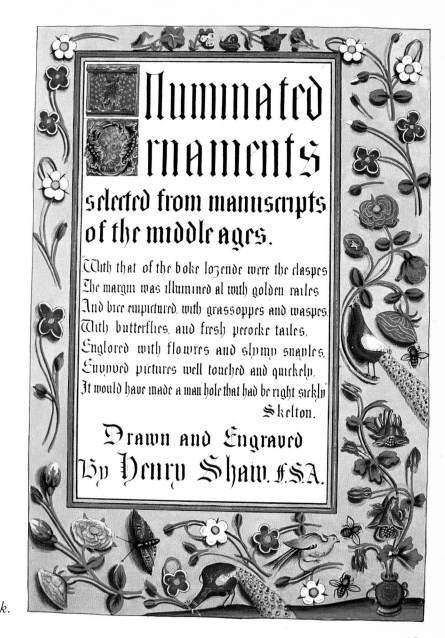

The title page of Henry Shaw's book.

THE ILLUMINATOR'S EQUIPMENT

Equipment can be very expensive and everyone has personal preferences, but a practising calligrapher will probably already possess most of the required items. If you are a complete beginner, it is a good idea to buy the minimum and select more sophisticated equipment after you have experimented a little and know what you feel most comfortable with and what works for you.

Drawing boards. For a novice, a strong piece of plywood will probably suffice. There are many different kinds of drawing boards on the market and you will be well advised to try several before selecting the type you buy. If you treat it with care, your drawing board will probably last you a lifetime.

A cutting mat made of a heavy plastic substance that appears to heal itself when you cut paper, board or vellum on it with a scalpel or a craft knife provides a good, non-slip surface to cut on and also prolongs the life of blades. However, such a cutting mat is rather expensive and you could use a heavy piece of cardboard or plywood as a substitute. *Never* cut on your drawing board or on a table top without ensuring that it is adequately protected.

Right. *The Victorians were fascinated by the wealth of ornamental sources brought to light by the great archaeological discoveries that took place in the nineteenth century. This plate shows decorative suggestions for the illuminator drawn from traditional Assyrian ornamental details.*

Exemple de Composition
pour l'Enluminure avec
les éléments de l'Art assyrien.

Les Documents contenus dans cette page sont tirés
de la galerie Assyrienne (Mission Dieulafoy) au Musée du Louvre.

Fragment de la frise des archers.

Réunion d'éléments assyriens,
formant bordure marginale, applicable
à l'enluminure.

17

Pencils. You will need a good range of pencils. Buy only good-quality drawing pencils. If you work on paper, the general-purpose HB type, the middle of the range between H (hard) and B (soft), will be good for most work, together with a B or a 2B to give a softer line. The softer grades of B smudge easily and you must keep a clean piece of paper under your hand to avoid spoiling your work.

If you work on vellum, use the very hard 6H, 3H or a 2H or at most an HB. Pencil smudges particularly easily on vellum and it is very difficult to clean it without damaging the vellum's fragile surface. To rule lines, calligraphers usually favour a very sharp, hard pencil (6H) and this is suitable for drawing on vellum.

Erasers. For pencil work on paper use soft rubber or vinyl. Erasures on vellum are always problematic. Try fresh white bread or gum rubber. The hard erasers that are available in pencil form to use on an old-fashioned typewriter can often be useful to remove small mistakes on vellum since they will not smear pencil marks.

Pens. Steel-nibbed, reed and quill pens all have their uses. Felt- or fibre-tipped pens are fun to play and experiment with, but these colours, like coloured inks, are not resistant to light and are therefore unsuitable for a piece of work that is intended to withstand the test of time.

Knives and scalpels. A well-made, solid pencil sharpener, free-standing or fixed to a worktop, with a receptacle to catch the shavings, is a useful piece of equipment, but when you work with the softest of pencils, in particular, you will need a razor-sharp knife to sharpen them.

A strong craft knife with replaceable blades is indispensable for cutting board as is a scalpel or X-Acto knife to erase colour from vellum and to cut paper or vellum pieces to size. A word of warning: never skimp with blades. Replace them as soon as they are blunt (they should cut a piece of paper all the way along the line in *one* clean stroke), and remember to dispose of blades safely. Never put them loose in a wastepaper basket.

You will also need a quill knife, which most calligraphers will already own.

Right. *Elements of Egyptian art drawn by Ernest Guillot from sarcophagi and other Egyptian artefacts displayed at the Louvre Museum.*

Tiré d'un pillier.

Décoration tirée d'un instrument de musique. (Musée du Louvre.)

Cadre de pectoral cloisonné. (Musée du Louvre.)

Colonne Egyptienne.

Bouquet peint tiré des hypogées.

Les motifs 1 à 9 sont en majeure partie tirés des boîtes à momies et sarcophages du Musée du Louvre.

19

Black outline of a Saxon initial.

Tube colours. Tube watercolours are convenient and will keep indefinitely, provided you close the tube as soon as you have squeezed the desired amount of paint onto a palette. These colours come already mixed and only require water to thin them.

Gouache. Gouache colours are also convenient to use, since they are ready mixed and are available in tubes or little pans. They are less subtle than watercolours, but their colours are very bright and they dry to a matt and opaque finish. They are particularly useful for large areas of colour.

Cake colours. Cake colours are sold in small china containers or as dry, small rectangles, wrapped in paper. The absence of glycerine in them means that they are less sticky than prepared watercolours and this may make them easier to use by those new to vellum. A wet brush will soften the surface of the cake and release the colour, but this is a slow process. Do not swamp the cake with water.

Powder colours. If you are a purist and wish to work in a way that is closer to the methods used by the medieval illuminator, these ready-ground pigments will give you pure and strong colours. However, they have to be fixed to the page by the use of a suitable medium such as egg yolk, gum water or glair.

Coloured inks. There is little use for coloured inks in illumination.

Brushes. Good brushes are expensive, but if well treated they should keep for years. Always wash them after use, reform the tips and dry upright in a jar. Old brushes can still be of use to load pens and to mix colour.

For watercolour painting, sable brushes cannot be surpassed. They are the most costly, but last the longest. Beginners can use squirrel or ox-hair brushes, but they lose their point faster than sable brushes and are not as supple and springy.

Brushes made of synthetic fibres do not hold colour as well as those made of natural hair.

Paper. Buy the best-quality paper you can afford for actual work and keep a cheaper stock for roughs. Semi-transparent layout paper is available in continuous rolls or in pads of varying sizes. It is useful for many things besides tracing.

Ivory card which has a smooth surface and is, although thin, quite firm, is useful to protect blank areas of your drawing as you are painting, to mix colours and to protect your work when you are not actually working on it. Sheets of white blotting paper are often handy to lay on a table top in a cramped area since they will absorb accidental spills. They also provide good padding material under paper or vellum while illuminating or painting.

Vellum. Vellum can be bought as a whole skin or cut to page size. For experimentation or for very small pieces of work, ask the supplier for off-cuts. Vellum is available in different weights and the nature of your work will dictate your choice of thin or heavier vellum. Even more than expensive handmade paper, vellum calls for careful storage (*see* section on vellum, page 35).

Drawing instruments. Steel rulers of different lengths, T-squares, a pair of compasses, dividers, set squares, and a few French curves for drawing flowing, rounded shapes, should also be part of your equipment.

Gold leaf and shell gold. Gold leaf comes in little books as transfer gold, in which the leaf is attached to a paper backing, and as loose leaf and is used in conjunction with gum ammoniac or gesso. Shell gold is sold as a powder and must then be mixed with the appropriate medium; it is also available ready mixed which makes it easier to use.

Agate burnisher. This tool is used in gilding and for punching little patterns in a flat gold background.

Other substances. Distilled water, gum arabic, gum water (a solution of gum arabic and water already mixed by the supplier), sandarac, pumice powder, glycerine and fresh egg may be needed depending on your working methods.

Miscellaneous. Clean rags, paper tissue, a small natural sponge, a supply of clean, clear glass jars, a palette or a number of white saucers in which to mix colours.

To stretch paper you will need brown paper tape (the kind you moisten with water). Masking tape which does not damage the surface of the paper is useful to hold work in position.

It is important to remember that many pigments and other dry colours are highly toxic and that they, as well as knives, blades and other sharp instruments, should be safely locked away when not in use, particularly if you have small children or pets in the house.

Left. *Saxon letters redrawn by Henry Shaw from manuscripts dating back to the latter half of the tenth century.*

Right. *Initials drawn from seventh-century manuscripts of the French Merovingian period (relating to the Frankish dynasty founded by Clovis I, AD 500 to 751). Their simplicity of shape and strong colours make them appealing and easy to copy. The early Christian symbol of the fish was a popular motif with illuminators.*

1.2.3. Motifs tirés des Extraits de St Augustin. (Bibl. nat. latin 2110.)

6. Initiale tirée d'un manuscrit latin N° 1732. (Bibl. nat.)

10. Q. Tiré d'un recueil de traité moraux. (Bibl. nat. lat. 1311.)

4. C et 5. I. Initiales mérovingiennes tirées de l'histoire des Francs par St Grégoire de Tours. (Bibl. nat. latin 132 bis.)

9. Lettre I également tirée du même manuscrit.

7. 8. E et D. Initiales mérovingiennes tirées d'un Commentaire de St Augustin. (latin 2706.)

A B C D

E F G H I J K L

M N O P Q R S

T U V W X Y Z

24

This form of black letters, or Gothic Church Text as it was often called, is still a popular alphabet today. The proportions must be studied carefully and the right amount of black to white spaces created when writing the letters. Note that the white space inside each letter is about equal to the area of black in the letter form. Care must be taken not to make these letters too large and open. For example, in the letters "M" and "N" the width between the vertical strokes is the same as the pen width of the strokes themselves. In the alphabet shown here, the pen angle is about 35 degrees for most strokes, but the angle is changed a little for parts of the "A", "G", "S" and "Z," as you will notice if you look closely.

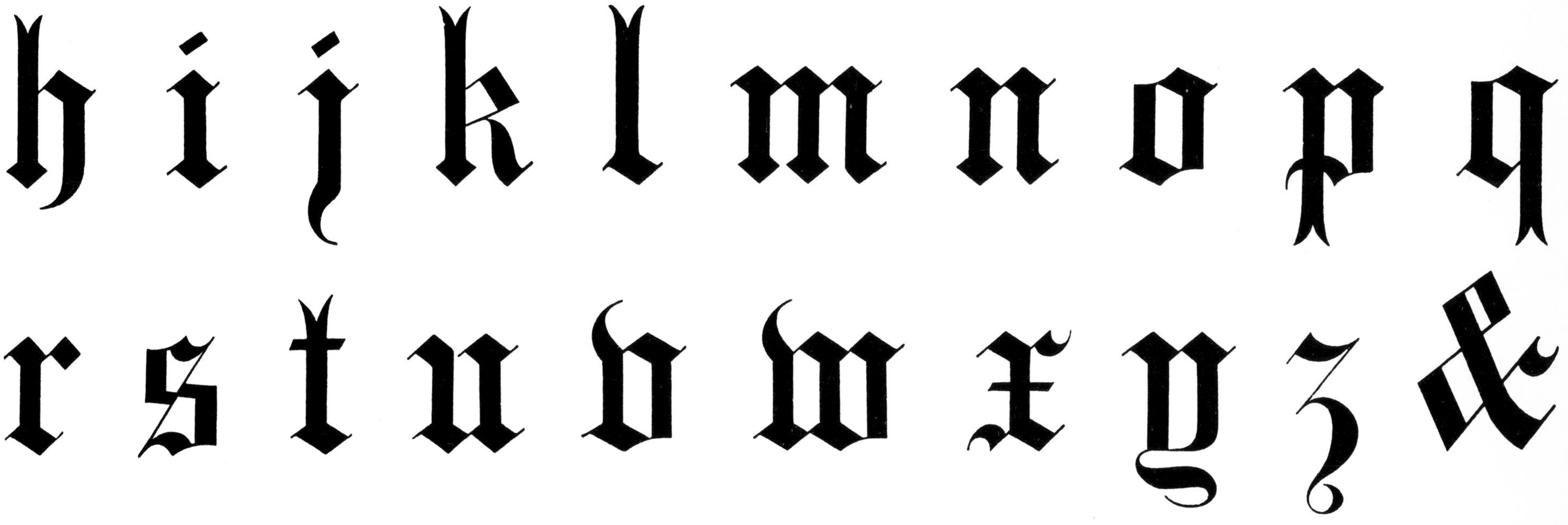

Pen Angle

abc defg
hijklmnopq
rstuvwxyz&

WORKING WITH PAPER, VELLUM & PARCHMENT

While you are experimenting and learning, most of your work will probably be on paper. You should use the best you can afford. Cheap paper is made of a mixture of rag and cellulose (wood pulp). Acid, which is often added to hasten the breaking down process of wood fibres, shortens the life of cheaper paper and it will quickly discolour and become brittle. The illuminator needs paper that will above all be strong and stable to take the weight of ink and watercolour, possibly on both sides of the sheet, without distorting or shrinking.

The best paper is handmade from linen rags. It is very expensive and difficult to obtain. The next best is paper made from cotton rags, or from a mixture of cotton and esparto grass. These papers can be hand- or machine-made. Handmade paper is, of course, the more expensive of the two. Handmade paper can be identified by the crinkly deckle edge left by the pan or "deckle" in which each sheet of paper is made. This characteristic can be used as a feature in a piece of work. Handmade papers have a watermark and its position indicates the right side of the paper. The surfaces are slightly different, but both sides are suitable for painting. Some of the best handmade papers and boards now come from Japan.

The paper you use should be light in colour and reflect light well. A beginner could use a good-quality cartridge paper that is suitable for painting on, but it must have a very smooth surface, if calligraphy is going to be included in the work. Some Fabriano papers are suitable for both illumination and calligraphy. These and other hot-pressed papers do not require any preparation other than stretching, for if it is a piece of work using large areas of very wet washes the paper would otherwise wrinkle.

Right. *Elements drawn from manuscripts of the eighth and ninth century. Details 7, 8, 9 and 10 are Celtic. The Carolingian period in France witnessed a tremendous growth of manuscript writing and of the arts in general, reaching its zenith during Charlemagne's reign (c AD 742-814).*

1. *Initiale symbolique d'après un ms. lat. 9388. (Bibl. nat. IXe S.)*

VER BUM

VISIO

VTI LAS

2.3.4. *Initiales d'un manuscrit lat. 5. (Bibl. nat.) IXe S.*

6. *Initiale tirée d'un Livre des évangiles. IXe S.*

7. 8. 9. 10. *Entrelacés celtiques d'un ms. latin 1203. (Bibl. nat.) VIIIe S.*

11. 12. 13. 14. *Chapiteaux et bases de Colonnes tirés du Codex aureus d'Ada, sœur de Charlemagne, conservé à Trèves.*

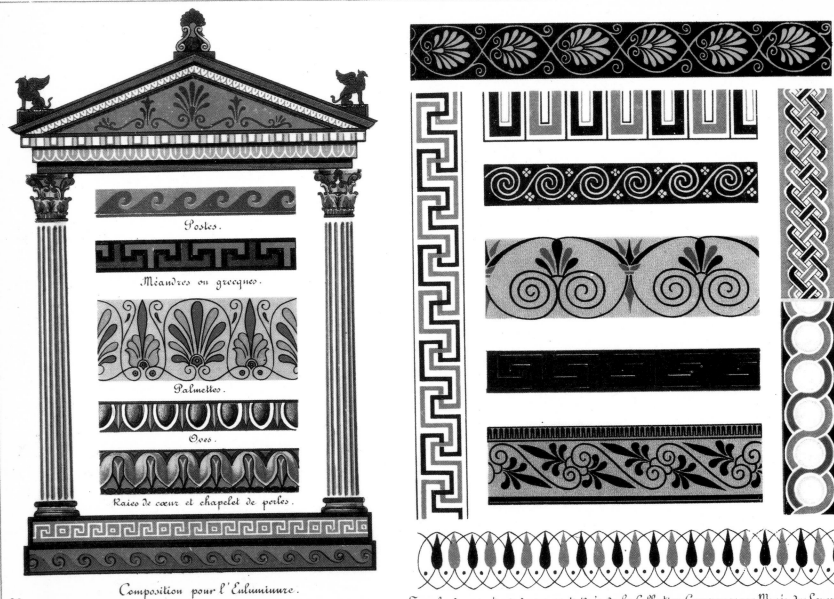

Postes.

Méandres ou grecques.

Palmettes.

Oves.

Raies de cœur et chapelet de perles.

Composition pour l'Enluminure.

Tous les documents ci-dessus sont tirés de la Collection Campana au Musée du Louvre.

The paper should be well sized, that is not too absorbent. Test this by putting a drop of water on the paper. It should not disappear too quickly into the surface.

The paper should never be waxy; imitation parchment and vellum paper, however tempting to a beginner, are particularly bad in this respect and should be avoided.

Stretching paper. If thin watercolour is used liberally over large surfaces, the paper will wrinkle when it dries. To prevent this, you must "stretch" your sheet of paper before painting. You will need a clean, smooth drawing board slightly larger than the paper to be treated and enough gummed paper tape 2 inches (50 mm) wide to hold down each side of the sheet.

Lay the paper to be stretched right-side up on the board.

Dampen the paper with a wet sponge. Do not overdo this.

Allow the water to soak into the paper for a few minutes. Smooth the paper gently, lifting and patting it to release large air bubbles.

Moisten four strips of gummed paper and place them along each side of the paper - half on the paper and half attached to the board.

Allow the paper to dry at room temperature. This may take several hours, depending on the thickness of the paper.

When working on a book, there is usually no need to stretch the paper, unless there will be large areas of watery washes. Unfortunately, while stretching provides an excellent surface to paint on, it is also a poor one for writing. Therefore, a sheet of paper that will be used for painting and writing, and requires stretching, would have to be stretched *after* the calligraphy has been done. In this case, stretching is best left to an expert because if the sheet is dampened too much, the non-waterproof ink used for the calligraphy may smudge. Painted initials as well as gilding should be done *after* stretching.

For fine illumination work, there is really no substitute for vellum or parchment. Since these materials are costly and require special treatment, it is best to practise on paper. As your working knowledge of illumination processes and techniques increases and your confidence and delight in the craft develop, you will certainly want to try your hand at working on vellum and parchment.

Left. *Greek architectural details for the use of illuminators.*

Détail de pilastre
du Jubé de la Cathédrale de Limoges

Sauf le N.º 1, tous les éléments composant cette
planche sont tirés des heures à l'usage de
Chartres, imprimés par Simon Vostre. 1501.
(Bibl. Nat. imp B. 575.)

The origins of vellum and parchment. Generally speaking, parchment is sheepskin or goatskin and vellum is cow or calfskin. Originally, however, it is doubtful if such a clearcut distinction was made. The word "parchment" derives from the name of Pergamum, an ancient city of Asia Minor, where the processing of sheep hides for writing on was perfected around 200 B.C., as well as the production of fine scraping tools. Vellum comes from the Latin word *vellus* – a fleece.

Lime was used to remove hair and fats from the animal hides to produce fine white skins. For extra fine parchment, the skins of unborn or stillborn animals were frequently used. Medieval parchments of this kind are as fine as tissue paper and have remained extremely flexible to this day.

The skins were stretched on frames or hoops, and scraped with special, semi-circular knives. This was often done by apprentices, but finished by the more skilled workers. The skins were then rubbed with lime or pumice to make them smooth. The lime, as an alkali, also drew out any excess fat.

The task of making parchment for high-quality books was enormous since relatively little of a whole skin could be used for a large double page. It was not uncommon for the skins of three hundred sheep to be needed for one copy of the Bible. These manuscripts are considered valuable today but, judged by the expense in man-hours, they were every bit as expensive in the Middle Ages.

Until the twelfth century, books were aimed at two main markets. One was the luxury trade for kings, princes and noblemen who usually wanted bibles, prayer books or books of hours. The other was the Church, which acted as patron and required books similar to those wanted by wealthy individuals.

Vellum and parchment, being organic materials, have qualities – the softness of the surface and the way in which they react to ink and colours – that are quite unique. The manufacture of vellum and parchment is now very limited and these products cannot be bought from art-supply shops and are only available from a few specialist outlets. You will find addresses in the List of Suppliers, page 140.

Left. *Sixteenth-century borders and motifs.*

31

If you buy your vellum already cut to page size, it will cost more, but you are also getting only the best part of the skin and no wastage. If you buy a whole skin, remember that the spine of the skin should run from the top to the bottom of your page. Check which is the hair surface of the vellum. This is the matt side and should feel almost like felt to the fingers. The flesh side is smoother and often shiny and you may encounter such problems as veins. By choice, the scribe works on the hair side, but this is not always possible when planning a book.

Fine vellum can be used as it is, but if you want to do particularly intricate work, you will have to prepare the surface.

Be careful not to "over-prepare" vellum. While a velvety, napped surface is fine to write on with a chisel-edged pen, for instance, it is no good at all for detailed painting. The brush is too soft to penetrate the nap and the colour just rolls off the surface. If you have to raise a nap, try to plan your work accurately on the page and treat only those areas intended for calligraphy.

Vellum comes in various weights. For small, delicate pieces of work, a very fine skin is perfect, while heavier, thicker parchments are more appropriate for book work and large wall hangings and scrolls.

Each skin is different: look for colours and markings which can add character to your finished piece of work.

Right. *Architectural details found in Chartres Cathedral in France (sixteenth century).*

I et II. Détails de la clôture du chœur de la Cathédrale de Chartres.

PREPARING VELLUM

Equipment you will need:
1) Straight-edged strip of heavy metal
2) Sharp, heavy-duty craft knife
3) Large piece of board or cutting mat

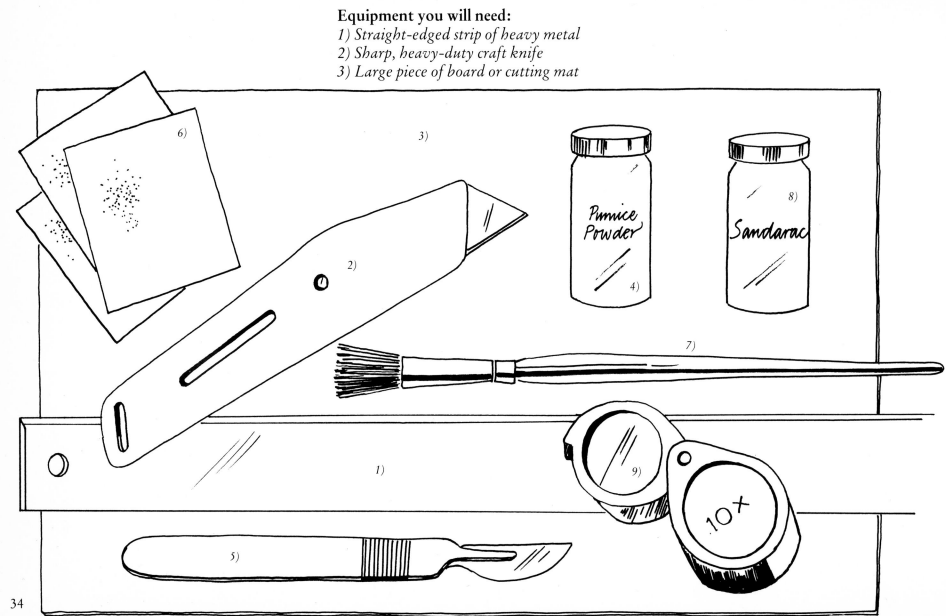

4) *Pumice powder*
5) *Scalpel or X-Acto knife with a sharp new blade*
6) *Fine-grade abrasive paper*
7) *Large soft brush*
8) *Powdered sandarac*
9) *Powerful magnifying glass*

Preparing the skin

1) Lay out the sheet of vellum, hair side uppermost.
2) Using a sharp knife or razor, remove any surplus roughness or lumps; scrape where necessary to encourage an even nap.
3) Using a pad of cloth, rub pumice powder over the skin.
4) Raise a nap by rubbing with fine dry abrasive paper.
5) Brush away all dust with a soft brush. (This is best done out of doors.)
6) Apply finely ground sandarac which will absorb any grease on the skin and help to ensure sharper, crisper pen strokes. It must be well rubbed in. Do not use too much sandarac, as it may clog the pen. Some scribes recommend using sandarac in a fine linen bag and dabbing it on the surface.
7) Brush away excessive pouncing with a soft brush.

Storing vellum and parchment. Since they are natural materials, vellum and parchment react to heat and humidity and it is important to remember this when storing them. Manufacturers keep their stock rolled up, although parchment can also be stored flat between boards. It is, however, vital that the room should not be damp, nor too warm either. Beware of central heating which has a drying effect.

While you are working on a piece, keep it flat between boards, using a weight if necessary; make sure, of course, that inks and colour are fully dry before covering.

If a piece of parchment has been kept rolled up for a long time, it will have developed a curl, making it difficult to work on. Leave it for a few hours in a slightly damp atmosphere to soften it, then wrap it gently round a large cardboard tube in the opposite direction to the curl for several more hours. The skin can then be flattened between boards.

Detail from a fifteenth-century manuscript. The careful shading on the flowers gives them an almost three-dimensional aspect. The gilded background has been scored with a tiny seed-like pattern that catches the light.

1.2. Encadrements tirés
du Livre des Quatre Evangiles.
(Bibl. nat. latin 266.)

3. Détail de bordure tiré
de la Bible de Charles le Chauve.
(Bibl. nat. latin 1.)

4. Chapiteau tiré du
Manuscrit N° 266.

5. Fragment de Cadre
tiré de la Bible de
Charles le Chauve.

Much still remains to be discovered about the way the early scribes and illuminators worked, although safer assumptions can now be made about their materials. We are fortunate that some modern scholars, Michael Gullick, for example, are also calligraphers; and some modern calligraphers, for example Sam Somerville, are also trained scientists. Michael Gullick is fairly certain that the work of producing books and manuscripts was shared, especially in the later Middle Ages when it would seem that teams of scribes and artists worked together, with various members specializing in either writing or laying on colour or gold, or drawing initial outlines for designs. In those days of intense religious fervour, it can be assumed that there was a unity of purpose that encouraged cooperation. At that time the production of books would have been regarded as a religious task for the glory of God rather than today's more egocentric view of art as self-expression.

Imagine the scriptorium of a European cathedral or monastery: a big open room, usually upstairs, with larger than average casements. Some early writers have described the beautiful natural light streaming through the unstained glass of the scribes' workshop windows. Apprentices would be everywhere – running errands, fetching clean water, gathering quills. Parchment or vellum would be stored on racks where it would not become either dry and brittle or damp and mildewed.

There would be as many as ten different craftsmen coming and going through the workshop. Local villagers would also be hired to do unskilled work when a big order for books was being filled. It is said that between five hundred and a thousand perfect sheepskins were needed for the Domesday Book and *The Book of Kells* used up the skins of more than three thousand cows.

Chief among the craftsmen would be the scribes themselves, who wrote the texts in the style particular to their own scriptorium. Of equal status would be the limners, or illuminators, who painted illustrations and decorated letters. Then there were turnours who specialized in drawing initial letters and the borders around the pages. Some workshops also employed rubricators, who at first literally added "rubrics" or red marginal writing, but soon became experts at laying in any colour, headings or additions. There were also miniators who were skilled in the use of cinnabar, a precious natural vermilion, which was mixed with red lead (minium); hence the name "miniator" and eventually the term "miniature" for the works they produced.

Left. *Carolingian period, ninth century, motifs drawn from bibles and contemporary manuscripts.*

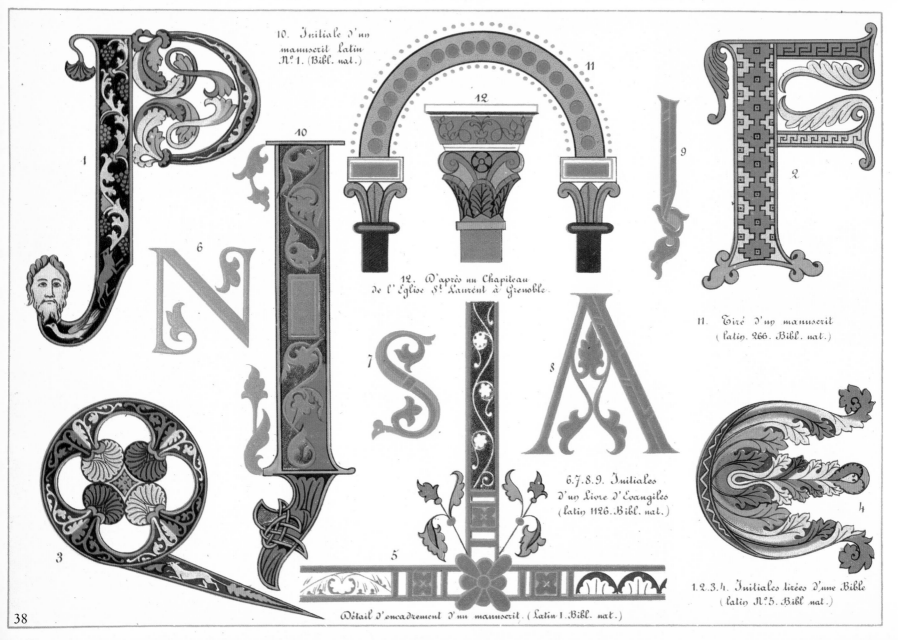

10. Initiale d'un manuscrit latin Nº 1. (Bibl. nat.)

12. D'après un Chapiteau de l'Église St Laurent à Grenoble.

11. Tiré d'un manuscrit (latin. 266. Bibl. nat.)

6.7.8.9. Initiales d'un Livre d'Évangiles (latin 1126. Bibl. nat.)

Détail d'encadrement d'un manuscrit. (Latin 1. Bibl. nat.)

1.2.3.4. Initiales tirées d'une Bible (latin Nº 5. Bibl. nat.)

Rich merchants also developed a taste for the beautifully crafted volumes and they, too, began commissioning books, as well as the Church and the nobility. As a result, the demand greatly increased and numerous workshops flourished between the twelfth and fourteenth centuries in Paris, Bologna, Oxford and York.

Parchment for books was originally "pricked out" with a needle for ruling up. This pricking through several sheets resulted in accurate line-guides on both sides for more than one page. Using the tiny holes, writing lines were ruled with a sharp piece of lead or a blunt iron point which left a furrow in the parchment surface. This gradually disappeared after the writing had been done. Sometimes metal comb-like tools were used to draw several lines at once.

By the nineteenth century, paper was the ground used for almost all work and only antiquarians and legal stationers were interested in parchment. Prior to the great revival of interest in medieval art, hundreds of parchment books and manuscripts had been destroyed, used in bookbinding or chopped up to make glue or size.

By 1906, Edward Johnston was complaining that the vellum specially sold for illuminators was quite unsuitable for the purpose, since it lacked that velvety nap which forms the perfect working surface. He recommended the best sheepskin, which was supplied by law stationers. Even better was lambskin. A superior quality made at that time was called Roman Vellum, said to be in imitation of the vellum used for Vatican documents. This material is no longer produced today to the consternation of professional illuminators.

Another ancient material which you may well wish to try is papyrus, made by pressing the fibres produced by soaking the leaves of the papyrus plant. The manufacture had dwindled but in recent years Egypt has reintroduced its production. Some lovely work can be produced on papyrus, using a reed pen.

Left. *Carolingian period, ninth century, initials and architectural details.*

INKS

Ink has been with us for a long time. The best writing fluids were designed to last many years and indeed they have: possibly the earliest ink known to scholars is on a 4,500-year-old Egyptian papyrus roll, now in Berlin. The earliest Greek writing in ink to be seen has lasted about 4,200 years. Any recipes which have withstood that test of time must be taken seriously.

Ink is usually defined as a fluid with which written records are made. This may be on papyrus, parchment, paper or similar material. Documents may be created by both writing and drawing. The tool used could be a brush, reed, quill or metal pen. Ink in diluted form was also used for preliminary outlines prior to painting or illuminating a manuscript. Inks may be fabricated in stick or tablet form similar to the watercolour tablets in children's paintboxes. This method was common in antiquity and is still the general practice in China today.

The earliest inks seem to have been processed from carbon (lamp black), red ochre or green malachite. They were always ground finely and usually compressed into sticks or cakes. Gum was added to encourage the pigment to emulsify, or suspend itself, in water and, to act as a fixative. Papyrus, probably one of the earliest writing surfaces, is much more porous than parchment and grainy or gummy inks were therefore quite acceptable, since they could soak into the papyrus and combine with it. Centuries later, if such gluey inks were used on the hard surface of parchment, they tended to harden, become brittle and crack off. For this reason, the more fluid oak-gall inks were technically preferable.

Being no longer portable in tablet form, these inks made from dyes and infusions were carried in stoppered animal horns hung from the scribe's belt. Later, small clay pots, glass bottles and pewter ink stands came into use. Until the invention of the fountain pen, writers had to carry their quills and ink around separately.

The early Latin word for ink was *atramentum* from *ater* – black. This probably

Right. *A delicate border and miniature drawn from a fifteenth-century French manuscript.*

Below. *Miniature drawn from a thirteenth-century French Psalter.*

Below. *This cipher of Charles V of France ("Karolus" is the Latin form of his name) is drawn from a fourteenth-century document. It demonstrates considerable skill in drawing, as fish and snakes and other creatures lend their shapes to letters. Medieval scribes frequently used such letters, although they could easily look grotesque today.*

described both inks made from carbon or soot and those made from the cuttlefish – sepia. Tyrian, a deep purple dye obtained from molluscs, was also used as ink.

The modern word "ink" derives from another Latin word: *encaustum* – "that which burns in." This did not mean that it burnt into the paper, but that the pigments were also used in pottery where they were "fired" into tiles and other ceramics.

Gold and silver inks made from finely ground metals are also described by Pliny; and Plutarch mentions the rubric or red ink from minium or vermilion.

By far the most common ink in Western European history is the *encaustum* made from tannin and copperas, that is tannin made from oak galls (the swelling in the bark of the oak tree) plus iron sulphate. Oak galls can be picked, usually in the late summer or autumn, and iron (or ferrous) sulphate, which is a dietary supplement, can be bought in most chemists or drugstores. Here is a simple recipe for making ink: place half a dozen oak galls into half a jam jar of rainwater. Drop in four or five small iron nails. Leave on a sunny windowsill for a week, by which time you will have ink. It can indeed be both fun and worthwhile experimenting with various recipes. Try mixing equal parts of powdered yellow ochre and ivory black with a small amount of vermilion (*see* pigment section, page 57). With the addition of a little gum arabic, this will make a fine traditional ink that will not fade even on prolonged exposure to light. There are no exact proportions for this ink – you will need to try it for yourself to see how it suits your purpose.

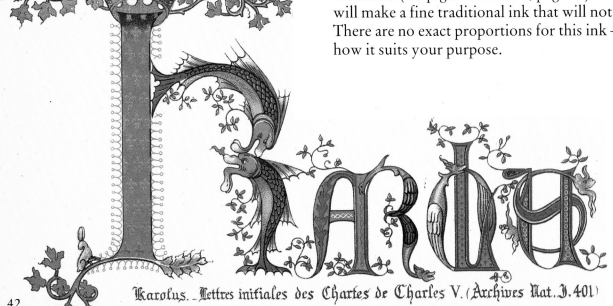

Karolus. Lettres initiales des Chartes de Charles V. (Archives Nat. J. 401)

Opposite. *This plate shows initials and motifs in the Romanesque style drawn from a number of Latin bibles of the twelfth century.*

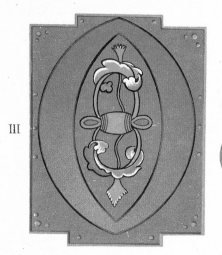

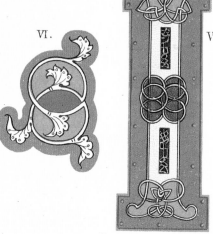

ON
FI
TE
MI
NI
DO
MI
NO

III. Initiale tirée d'une Bible latine,
de la Bibl. nat. (latin 8.)

IV et V. Initiales. Style Anglo-Saxon, tirées
d'une Bible latine. (Bibl. nat. latin 8.)

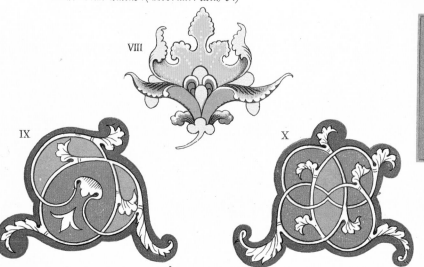

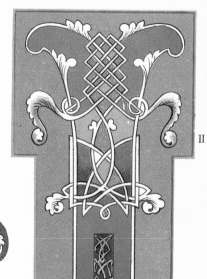

I. Initiale tirée d'un Nouveau Testament,
de la Bibl. ngl. (latin 254.)

VI à X. Éléments d'ornementation tirés
des Initiales d'une Bible de la Bibl. nat.

II. Fragment de Bordure tiré d'un nouveau
testament de la Bibl. nat. (lat. 254.)

Today many types of ink are available from art-supply shops and stationery stores. For the calligrapher, non-waterproof, carbon-based inks are best. They are specially designed for drawing and calligraphy and should not be used in a fountain pen. They are a denser black than everyday inks. I recommend Winsor & Newton's non-waterproof India ink. Avoid ordinary India ink containing gum arabic: it is too shiny and forms a brittle crust when dry. One of the best calligrapher's inks, which is available in the United States, is Higgins' non-waterproof. Chinese stick ink, rubbed down on a slate with rainwater or distilled water, is also very good. It is obtainable from most art-supply shops.

Do not use coloured inks for calligraphy or illumination – they are transparent and waterproof. For coloured writing, use gouache colours mixed to a consistency that will run in your pen. They give a good, solid colour and do not fade in the light. You will need to experiment to get the right consistency. If the mixture is too thick, it will clog the pen.

Right. *Detail and floral border from fifteenth-century French manuscripts.*

Tiré d'un manuscrit de la Bibl. de l'Arsenal. Mᵉ 639.

Bordure et Médaillons tirés des Heures illuminées   1.2.3. Fleurons tirés de la Toison d'or
(Bibl. Nat. Latin 1173)   (Bibl. Nat. Franc. 331)

En-tête de Chapitre tiré du manuscrit Grec N.º 139.
(Bibl. nat. X.º Siècle.)

En-tête de Chapitre — Du manuscrit N.º 139.

En-tête de page. Manuscrit N.º 139.

Composition pour l'enluminure par la juxtaposition des éléments byzantins de 1 à 5, tirés du manuscrit 139.

Cartouche formant en-tête de Chapitre. Manuscrit 139.

Initiale byzantine.

Fragment d'encadrement N.º 139.

Angle de Cadre tiré du Manuscrit grec 543. (Bibl. nat.)

En-tête de page.

COLOUR

Below. *This enlarged detail from a border in a fifteenth-century manuscript shows clearly the stage of manuscript decoration at that time. It alternates between the realism of earlier works, as shown in the beautifully observed pea-flowers and pods, and the growing formalism of the foliage which completes the pattern. Yet the design hangs together in a pleasantly unified way.*

Cultivating a colour sense is essential for successful illumination. Whether you wish to produce work in the spirit of a particular period or evolve your own colour associations within traditional or contemporary designs, the more you learn about the way colours interact with one another, the more pleasing your work will become. The medieval illuminators used strong colours – red, blue, green and purple hues with gold and silver. Yet with this somewhat restricted palette, they created works of intense and lasting beauty. The glowing and full-bodied colours allied themselves well to the bold shapes of mythical beasts and stylized foliage that featured prominently in their work. On the other hand, they also frequently introduced naturalistic details of plants and animals and in this case they delighted in rendering all the delicacy of colour required by their subject. Look, for instance, at the delicately formed pea flowers and pods shown in the detail on the right. Many pages from medieval manuscripts appear to have fresh natural flowers strewn on their formal gilded borders.

The medieval illuminator was bound by the traditions of his particular scriptorium and the conventions of his period. The calligrapher of today knows no such restrictions. When working on broadsheets and broadsides, it is important that they harmonize with their surroundings. When devising your own colour schemes, do not make them too elaborate. Remember that the aim of illumination is to enhance the text and draw the eye to the features you wish to emphasize. Within this book you will find several predrawn "pages" or "frames" into

Left. *This plate groups Byzantine elements, mostly chapter heads and corners of borders, from tenth-century manuscripts.*

which you can introduce your own favourite poem or quotation. In each case, suggestions for illuminating the borders have been provided. Do not follow them slavishly: each of these drawings would lend itself to a dozen different treatments.

To develop and enhance your sense of colour, much may be gained from studying the work of Chinese and Japanese calligraphers in which calligraphy and drawing as well as subtle colour schemes play an integral part in the representation of an idea. Cultural associations, individual temperament and personal taste all contribute to the emotional response many of us have towards colours and their usage in a piece of work, as well as in our environment.

Effects of colour. Colours reflect light according to the type of pigment and surface used. Thus an ultramarine pigment used in a watercolour wash on white paper will give an entirely different effect from that of an ultramarine in an oil medium, painted on canvas. The visible effect of any colour is also altered by the proximity of other colours and by areas of black and white.

There are four generally accepted effects which I have found useful to remember:
Gold and strong bright blue always go well together.
When blue and red are painted side by side, the blue will always appear bluer and the red brighter and more scarlet.
When red and green are painted side by side, the red appears more crimson and the green more blue.
Black outlines around colours make them seem brighter.

Describing colours. The name of the colour – red, blue, green, yellow – is its hue. If you add white to the hue, you have a tint, whereas adding a black or another very dark colour to a hue gives you a shade. (Brown, for instance, is a shade of orange.) Warm and cold colours refer to the way colours group themselves according to their closeness in hue, tint or shade to blue (cold) or red (warm).

Primary, secondary and tertiary colours. Red, yellow and blue are primary colours. They cannot be obtained by mixing other colours together. Secondary colours consist of two primaries mixed together: blue and yellow, for example, produce green. Tertiary colours are made by mixing three or more colours together. Mixing the three primaries, for example, produces a neutral grey.

Complementary colours. The complementary of a colour is the primary that remains after mixing two together: red and yellow make orange; blue is then the complementary of orange. If you paint complementary colours of the same tonal value next to each other they will intensify each other and appear to vibrate.

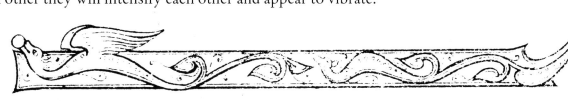

Modern pigments. On page 53 the traditional dry ground pigments closest to the ones the medieval illuminator would have used are listed. However, it is much easier, particularly for the beginner, to work with cake colours or with watercolours which come already mixed to the right consistency with an appropriate binding medium. You do not need *all* the colours listed below: those starred could form a basic palette. They are all stable and permanent colours suitable for use on paper or vellum.

*Yellow Ochre	Phthalocyanine Blue
*Cadmium Yellow Pale	*Prussian Blue
Naples Yellow	Cerulean Blue
Mars Yellow	*Viridian Green
*Cadmium Orange	Phthalocyanine Green
*Vermilion	*Winsor Violet
Indian Red	*Chinese White
*Cadmium Red	Titanium White
*French Ultramarine	*Ivory or Lamp Black
Cobalt Blue	Mars Black

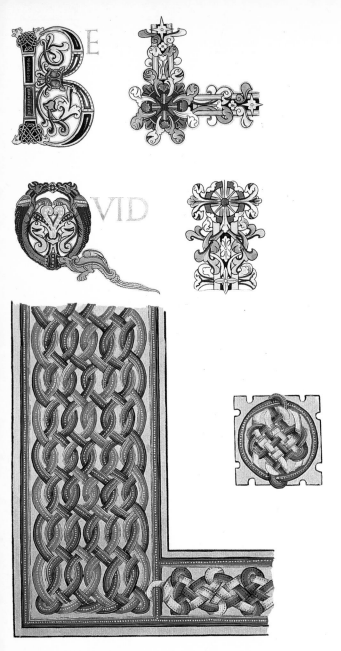

Points to remember. Vermilion has always featured prominently in the illuminator's palette. This colour has the unfortunate tendency to blacken when exposed to sunlight. Cadmium Red can be substituted for Vermilion but it also reacts adversely if painted next to one of the "copper-based" colours such as Emerald Green, causing the paints to blacken where they touch.

French Ultramarine is resistant to light. It is a good idea to mix it with another blue such as Cobalt and/or Cerulean. Cerulean Blue has a greenish tinge which does not make it very pleasing on its own, but it is very useful for mixing with other colours and blues. Adding it to Lemon Yellow will produce a good turquoise. Prussian Blue looks strong by itself, but it will strengthen and liven other blues and produces potent greens when mixed with yellow. Prussian Blue should always be used sparingly as it tends to dominate all other colours.

Viridian is a permanent, transparent copper green. It does not react adversely with other colours and it is not poisonous. A small amount of Chinese White will give it opacity and produce a useful green, not unlike Emerald Green which is highly poisonous and incompatible with some colours.

Top left. *Saxon letters and borders. They show the typically elegant patterns prevalent in Saxon manuscripts written in the latter half of the tenth century.*

Left. *Detail from an arabesque border and initial letter from a fifteenth-century Italian manuscript.*

Opposite page. *Byzantine motifs.*

1. 2. Motifs tirés d'un manuscrit grec, N°. 64. (Bibl. nat.)
1 bis et 2 bis ensembles.

Cadre d'un manuscrit grec N°. 79. (Bibl. nat.)

Initiale composée d'éléments byzantins.

3. 4. 5. 6. 7. 8. Fragments de cadres et têtes de chapitres
tirés d'un manuscrit grec. N°. 139. (Bibl. nat.)

Burnt Sienna, Raw Umber, Burnt Umber and Indian Red are all good reliable earth and safe colours from which to mix browns and greys.

Most major manufacturers of artists' paints produce booklets about the properties of the pigments and colours that they make. It is always worthwhile collecting them.

Unless you already have had a lot of experience of painting, do practise mixing your colours together. You will want to create your own shades. Keep records of your experiments, detailing the quantities of each colour used. When planning a piece of work, it is important to try your colours on a piece of the paper or vellum you plan to use and see how they react.

Gouache. Gouache colours are ideal for writing in colour in a piece of illumination. They are also perfect for painting large initial letters and heraldic subjects that require strong, opaque colours. Their opacity also means that they will cover a mistake which transparent watercolours do not. Gouache can be used in combination with watercolour, and their solid colours mix well with gilding (raised or shell gold).

Applying colours. When laying colour on paper or vellum, it is important to keep the colours flat and not to overload your brush. Watercolours are transparent and this characteristic can be exploited to great effect by applying thin layers of paint over each other. Always allow one layer to dry thoroughly before adding another.

If you study the illustrations from Guillot's book you will notice two main styles of manuscript painting. The earlier works dating from the fifth to the tenth centuries show flat colours with little or no shaded work. The later manuscripts, from the twelfth to the fifteenth century, are richer, and have highly elaborate gold decoration. The painted subjects are worked over so as to suggest a three-dimensional, solid image. Hairline finishings and outlines help to reinforce the richness of the colouring and gilding. Shading, white highlights and black outlines are used to great effect.

Try your hand at this work by copying the colour detail reproduced on page 35, for example. Disregard the gilded background for this exercise. First paint the lighter shades of green, red and blue on the leaves and flowers. Gradually build up your tones, shading them carefully. Add the highlights on the flowers and leaves. Do not apply pure white, but add a dab of the ambient colour before highlighting. Pure white would look too harsh against the rich colours. Last, apply the black outlines.

Ancient pigments. A list of some of the most ancient pigments and their properties is given below. This is not merely of historical interest, for it shows clearly the technical reasons for certain colours being retained by modern illuminators. The search for important modern substitutes, such as French Ultramarine for Lapis Lazuli, has always been motivated by the value and popularity of these original colours.

Aurum Mussivum. Bi-sulphide of tin, a golden brown of medium intensity, tempered with egg white. It is a metallic powder of complex composition and quite difficult to make. In medieval times it was used as an alternative pigment to gold itself, often around page borders. Its common name was Mosaic Gold. The equivalent substance today is bronze powder.

Brazilwood Lake. Known in Europe since antiquity, this is a blood-red vegetable extract also used to make dyes. Edward Johnston recommended stewing the powder and mixing it with carbonate of potash to obtain a purple stain for parchment. The colour has now been replaced by modern alizarin pigments or dyes.

Byzantium Purple. Also known as Tyrian Purple, Grecian Purple and Ostrum, the Imperial Purple of Rome. It is a pigment and a dye made from crushing up two Mediterranean shellfish (*Murex trunculis* and *Murex brandaris*). The Byzantium purple was slightly bluer than the Roman. In 1904, a purple coal-tar derivative was discovered which was identical in colour and much cheaper to produce.

Cinnabar. Native European Vermilion. Found as an ore containing sulphide of mercury, it is said that cinnabar mines in Spain are possibly three thousand years old. According to Theophrastus, the ore was sometimes obtained from inaccessible cliffs by shooting arrows at it to dislodge it. Cinnabar was often adulterated by the Romans with red lead (minium) to make it less costly.

Dragon's Blood. A ruby-red resin from the fruit of an Asiatic tree and used since

Below. *This letter has been enlarged to show its details clearly. The delicate tendrils are typical of the style: the letters would look equally good painted or gilded, the tendrils being added with a fine pen.*

Roman times. It comes mainly from Singapore in cylindrical sticks but it has been replaced nowadays by the preferable Alizarin Crimson.

Gamboge. A native transparent yellow gum from Thailand. Although not permanent, nor a true pigment, it is listed because it is so well known and was used from medieval times until the nineteenth century. Its place has now been taken by Cobalt Yellow for permanence.

Terre Verte. A native clay, coloured by traces of iron and manganese. It is found in parts of Czechoslovakia, Austria, Italy and Cyprus and is known variously as Tyrolean Green and Verona Green. It is transparent and has been widely used in Italy since earliest times. It is good for watercolour glazes and washes, and is quite permanent.

Kermes. A Crimson Lake made from crushed insects, and known to the Romans and medieval scribes. It is similar to Dragon's Blood in many ways and was used in the eighth century in *The Book of Kells*.

Madder Lake. Rose Madder – probably introduced into Europe by the Crusaders. Made from the crushed root of the madder plant. Greeks and Romans used it as a textile dye. Today, it has been replaced by shades of Alizarin.

Malachite. A native basic carbonate of copper and, according to the calligrapher Dorothy Hutton, "a splendid and luminous" green. It is similar to Emerald Green but is not as poisonous.

   An ancient pigment which is hard to obtain. It should be tempered with size when used. An artificial version called Bremen Blue was developed in the eighteenth century. Viridian is probably the most useful modern substitute although some scribes also recommend Chromium Oxide Green.

Right. *This plate shows a widely used style of lettering that appeared throughout Europe in the thirteenth century. This alphabet is continued on pages 58, 62, and 63.*

Naples Yellow. Lead antimonate. It is poisonous and ranges from a greeny-yellow to an orange yellow. Always popular with artists for flesh colouring. It has a tendency to turn green on contact with an iron or steel knife or spatula, so bone or wood were used. It dates back to the fifth century B.C.

According to Cennino Cennini, author of the earliest Italian treatise on painting, *Il Libro dell'Arte*, it was the volcanic earth from Vesuvius, hence the name. It is permanent and pleasant, and is still widely obtainable.

Orpiment. Yellow sulphide of arsenic widely used in *The Book of Kells* in place of gold. It is very beautiful and has a sparkly quality which reinforces the illusion of gold. It was sometimes given the name "King's Yellow" because of its valuable properties. It has been used since the very earliest of times. A reddish-orange version known equally as long was called Realgar. They are both very poisonous and also corrosive. They can attack other colours and even the substances used to bind colours.

The early scribes knew the properties of this colour well and took care to paint lines or "fences" of inert pigments around it to protect the colours next to it. It was abandoned in the nineteenth century because of its poisonous nature. It has become obsolete, and is mostly replaced today by Cadmium yellows.

Sandaraca. An antique term sometimes used rather confusingly by the Greeks and Romans for Orpiment, Realgar and Cinnabar. Gum Sandarac is an important resin used by scribes today and since medieval times; it is important to distinguish between them. Gum sandarac is a pounce brushed onto parchment or paper to repel ink and help make crisp fine pen lines.

Ultramarine. The ground semi-precious stone Lapis Lazuli from Afghanistan, Iran, China and Chile. It is a rich deep blue whose use as a pigment in Europe dates from around the twelfth century. The phrase "true blue" is said to arise from the use of this beautiful colour, which was more expensive than gold, for painting the robes of the Virgin Mary. Since 1828, Ultramarine has been produced artificially and is not as permanent as the genuine pigment. The artificial colour was discovered accidentally as a blue encrustation inside a furnace producing soda ash. It is known as French Ultramarine and is widely available today.

Verdigris. Green hydrated copper acetate, sometimes called Spanish Green. This is the substance found on copper roofs and pipes and collected by artists since Roman times. In the Middle Ages verdigris was dissolved in pine balsam. It will react chemically with a number of other pigments, especially those containing lead. It was widely used in *The Book of Kells*, and although it has the reputation of eating holes through parchment, it has not spoiled that manuscript. Today its colour can be matched by using Viridian as a starting point. Less subtle, but clearer greens can also be obtained using Phthalocyanine Green which was synthesized in 1938 and is extraordinarily permanent.

Vermilion. Mercuric sulphide, an opaque bright pure red and the heaviest of pigments. The earliest European use of Vermilion was probably in the eighth century. Vermilion was used unmixed to paint blood. Very small amounts can make almost any colour pinker or warmer, so it is a most valuable pigment. It will, however, turn black on contact with copper-based colours and is not very resistant to light.

   The best grades were always made in China, England or France. Before its introduction to Europe, Cinnabar was used.

   Sticks of Chinese Vermilion may be obtained today from Hong Kong or China and are attractive and easy to use, although quite expensive. An excellent modern substitute is Cadmium Red which comes in various shades.

Yellow Ochre. Clay coloured by iron deposits, this pigment has been used since antiquity and is completely permanent. It was used by cave painters in prehistoric times.

   The finest ochre is from France and is labelled J.F.L.S. which stands for *Jaune, fin, lavé, surfin* (yellow, washed and refined several times). The modern equivalent to ochre is Mars Yellow which is also an oxide of iron, but is artificially produced. Genuine ochre is still available, and generally preferred by illuminators.

Tiré du Psautier latin Nº 10.435 — Bibl. Nat.

Almost all the early pigments described here were known to the Victorians through translations of Cennini's *Libro dell'Arte* by Mrs Merrifield in 1844 and by Victor Mottez in 1858. The earliest English book to deal with the practical side of illumination was *The Arte of Limming*, printed in 1573, its author unknown. It contains several recipes for sizes and colours, and instructions for laying on gold and silver. A facsimile edition was reprinted by the Society of Scribes and Illuminators in 1979 and is still available.

Using dry pigments. Dry colours are available from reliable artists' supply shops and are sold in small glass tubes which are best kept in a flat box lined with cotton wool. To prepare your colours you will need a frosted-glass mixing slab, a small glass muller, and a china container to preserve each colour after it is mixed. A china palette that has a number of small wells with lids can be used. Such a palette is particularly good since it will keep the individual colours moist. If your palette does not have wells with lids, a small sheet of glass can be used. Enamel and plastic palettes are also available, but china is the best. You will also need a glass stopper or an agate pestle to mix the powder with the binding medium.

Unlike prepared watercolours, cake or pan colours or gouaches that only require the addition of water, powdered colours need to be bound together by a suitable medium, otherwise they would simply dust off the page when dry. There are various binding media for which recipes are given below and your choice will be dictated by personal preference, since each has different properties that bring their own characteristics to the work. Here again, experimenting with different media is the only reliable way to discover what you like to work with. But whatever binding agent you select, it must be thoroughly blended with the pigment to prevent the colour from flaking off. Similarly, the medium should not be so thick as to dry to a crust which would then crack. Experience rather than exact measurements will be the means to success.

A reliable medium is gum water, which has been used by illuminators since the eleventh century. Gum water can be bought, but is likely to contain some acid to deter mould. In the long run this may react adversely with sulphur and copper colours. To make your own gum water mix 1 part gum arabic, 2 parts water. Allow to dissolve; several hours later, strain through a piece of muslin and add a small amount of preservative such as naphthol dissolved in boiling water. This gum water can be kept in a tightly covered glass jar and diluted with water to the required strength.

Using gum water. In an egg cup, mix 1 part water to 2 parts gum water. These proportions may vary and you will have to do a test on a scrap of the paper or vellum you will use for the work. Too much gum will prevent the colour from flowing from the pen or brush, too little and the pigment will not be held by the medium. When you have done your test and the colour is fully dry, gently rub your finger across it to make sure the colour will not peel or dust off. Remember that gum-water medium is not waterproof and if you paint a further coat on, as may well occur in illumination, the base coat may move. Some recipes suggest the addition of a little sugar or honey.

Glair. This is made with the white of one egg beaten to a stiff foam (you should be able to turn the bowl upside down without the egg white moving). Leave overnight. The resulting liquid can then be used with the addition of a little honey, sugar or size to counteract the glair's strong tendency to contract when it has dried.

Glair and gum. Prepare the glair, but instead of adding honey, sugar or size, mix in ½ teaspoon of gum arabic, ½ teaspoon French white wine vinegar: dissolve and strain. Add ¼ teaspoon sal ammoniac dissolved in a little warm water and strain. Dissolve with distilled water before using. Glair and gum as a medium was advocated by Ida Henstock, the twentieth-century scribe noted for her traditional gilding.

Yolk of egg. This medium works best for illumination, rather than lettering, because the yolk is too thick to run off the pen easily. Separate the egg yolk carefully and remove the yolk-sac. Mix the egg yolk with about a third of its quantity of distilled water. Mix well before use. This medium dries slowly but hardens to a tough surface. Because of the high fat content, it sometimes has a shiny surface. If this occurs, add more distilled water. Any yellow tinge from the egg will soon disappear. It is an excellent medium for modelling, giving solidity to the shapes, and coats can be superimposed safely.

Mixing pigments and medium. Place a small quantity of powdered colour on your frosted-glass slab. Add a few drops of your chosen medium and grind gently with the glass muller. Using a palette knife, transfer the colour to a small jar or one of the wells in the palette. If the powdered colour that you bought appears to have been ground finely enough – and remember that the success of painting with dry colours rests to a large extent with the quality of the grinding of individual pigments – you can mix powder and medium directly on the palette. The obtained paint should, in either case, stay fresh from a few hours to two days, depending on the room's temperature. Cover when not in use.

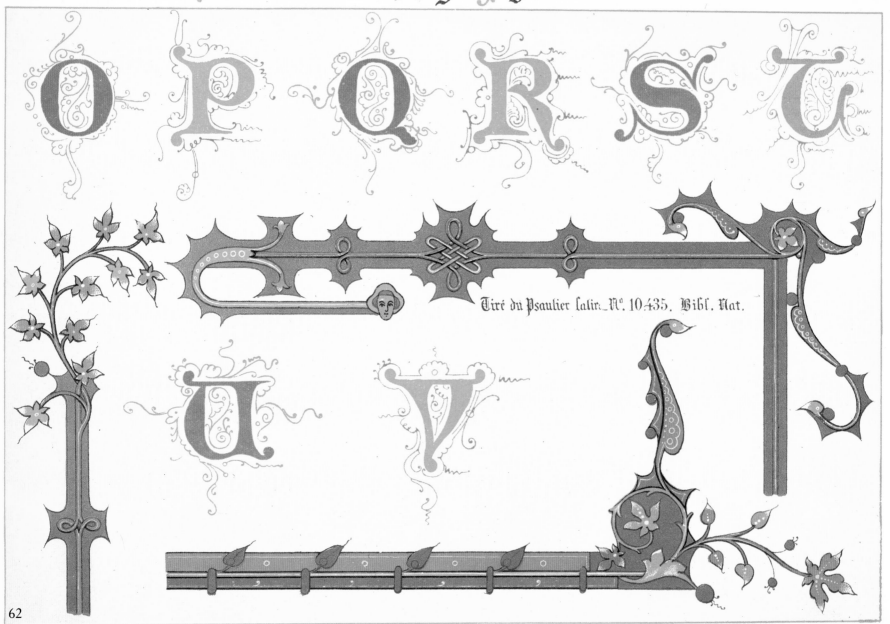

Tiré du Psautier latin. Nᵒ. 10435. Bibl. Nat.

Tiré d'une Bible latine N° 14.770. Bibl. Nat.

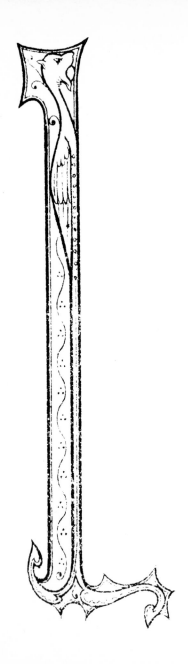

PENS & BRUSHES

Today most scribes use metal pen nibs, although for some the qualities of the goose or turkey quill are such that they are preferred for certain work such as laying on gesso or with colours that might react with metal.

The best nibs today are made by Wm. Mitchell and Hunts. Some fountain pens come equipped with lettering nibs, but in general they do not work as well as a dip pen that has a nib fitted with a slip-on reservoir.

For drawing the outlines of decorated pages, foliage and scrolls, a range of metal nibs and a firm wooden holder is recommended. Fine mapping pens are useful; they often come with the nibs already fitted into handles.

With a square-cut or chisel-nib pen, the edge rather than the point is used for writing. The pointed nib is a relatively new invention and was developed more as a tool to imitate the lines made by engravers than as a writing instrument. The original reed and quill pens of the Middle Ages were cut off to an edge; the rediscovery of this fact in the nineteenth century led to the development of the modern chisel nib used by most Western calligraphers today.

To work well, nibs must be kept clean. After use, a nib should be rinsed under running water, dried, and put away.

Nibs may be cut straight across or oblique right or left:

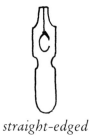

straight-edged

left oblique

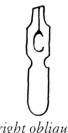

right oblique

Left oblique nibs are useful for left-handed scribes and for Arabic or Hebrew writing. The right oblique nib is useful for writing the uncial or half uncial style where the angle of the thick and thin strokes is nearer parallel to the writing line than the 30 degrees of many other hands.

Using a right oblique nib.

A slip-on ink reservoir underneath the nib is essential so that you will not run out of ink in the middle of letters. The most convenient type of reservoir is the small brass one made by Wm. Mitchell and Hunts – the Speedball. To increase the ink flow, slide the reservoir forward on the nib; to decrease the ink flow, slide it back. Nibs with fixed reservoirs do not allow for this adjustment. It is generally neater and cleaner to fill the reservoir using a small paintbrush full of ink rather than to dip the whole nib and reservoir into the bottle.

To obtain a crisper writing edge you may find it useful to sharpen your metal nibs on a fine Arkansas stone. This is done in exactly the same way as sharpening a small chisel.

Reed pens. It is just as easy to cut a reed pen and proceed to write with it as it was three thousand years ago. William Blake, the poet and painter, wrote:

> And I made a rural pen,
> And I stained the water clear,
> And I wrote my happy songs
> Every child may joy to hear.

His "rural pen" was probably a simple hollow reed with the nib cut at a slant. The most commonly used reed is the *Phragmites communis* that grows in swamps and shallow waters.

A reed pen.

Bamboo pens. If your garden, or a friend's, has a bamboo plant, you could make yourself a fine, serviceable pen which may last for months. Cut a piece of green bamboo about the length and thickness of a pencil and when it dries cut a nib. It may be stiffer and less responsive than a reed pen, but it is still worth making. There is no need to cut an ink slit in reed or bamboo because the grain of the stalk will act as a conductor for the ink. It is best to let the pen soak in ink for a little while before using it to assist this process of capillary action.

Reeds came before quills. In fact the Latin word *calamus* for reed became translated into the old English "quylle" which also means a reed. The correct name for the feather writing instrument is, of course, "pen" from the Latin *penna* describing the five outer wing feathers of the goose, swan, crow, raven or whatever was used at the time.

Quills. The most common pen in Europe has always been the goose quill. The goose was a widely kept domestic bird, and until the turkey was discovered in America, the goose quill provided the majority of pens. Turkey quills, which are a little tougher, began to become popular in Europe and many millions were imported in the seventeenth and eighteenth centuries. The effort of constantly cutting, trimming and recutting worn quills was always a problem and the search for a more permanent metal pen had gone on since Roman times. Gold pens were certainly known by the sixteenth century.

Left. *Alphabet drawn from an embroidered altar cloth belonging to the Church of St. Mary, Soest in Westphalia, Germany.*

Opposite. *A selection of sixteenth-century decorative elements.*

Château d'Anet

Tous les éléments de cette feuille
sont tirés des Grandes Arabesques
de du Cerceau. (Bibl. nat. Estampes
6ᵉ Vol. Ed. 2 g.)

Eglise St Maclou
à Rouen

For the scribe, quills still offer special advantages and one should know how to cut them. Today, it has become quite difficult to obtain turkey or goose feathers since modern plucking and bird-preparation processes often involve the mechanical destruction of the quills or their immersion in hot wax. If you can discover a farm or other source of supply, my advice is to keep quiet about it and collect as many for yourself and your friends as you can.

Detail from the rose window at the Sainte Chapelle in Paris.

Preparing and cutting a quill. To make quills harder and more suitable for writing, it is best to cure and temper them for use. This is done by soaking the feathers in water for about twelve hours after first cutting off the sealed end of the barrel at a slant to allow the water to reach the area where the shaft begins. Tear off the feather barbs by ripping them downwards from the flight end. Remove all surplus membrane from inside and outside the quill with tweezers, a hook or a narrow blade. Pour hot sand (fine silver sand heated on a baking tray in a warm oven for half an hour) into the barrel of the quill. To ensure it fills it up, stick the quill into hot sand so that it is being heated inside and out. The barrel should be completely covered up to the shaft. After a second or so, remove the quill and examine it. If it is blistered or distorted, the sand is either too hot or the quill was in it for too long. If the quill has not hardened after cooling, the sand was either not warm enough or the quill was removed too quickly. It is very much a process of trial and error. When the quill has been successfully cured, empty the sand and try cutting the nib. Quills have to be cut with a penknife. Most modern penknives are only "pocket knives." The penknife must have a strong, thick and short blade, preferably rounded on one side. This enables the scooping movement for the sides of the nib to be more easily cut. The handle should be large and chunky to hold, for considerable force and twisting action will be used while cutting the nib.

Initial drawn from a twelfth-century manuscript.

69

Right. *Details from fifteenth-century borders. The gilded chevron technique is typical of the period.*

Below. *Enlarged detail from a Byzantine border showing the use of simple geometric and repeat patterns.*

1.2. Tiré d'un Manuscrit de la Bibl. Nat.
(Français N° 2678)
3.4.5. Détails de Bordures tirés
d'un Manuscrit de la Bibl. Nat. (Franc. 541)

6.7. Tirés des Heures de N.D.
(Lat. 1166. Bibl. Nat.)

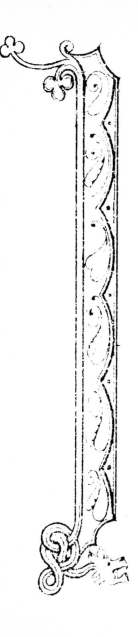

GILDING

"Illumination" is the reflection of light on gold leaf. In dark old monasteries and churches, the gilded letters reflected the candlelight in the evenings and enhanced the sacred character of the holy texts they decorated. In our more materialistic times, you are more likely to be using illumination to ornament a favourite poem or for a commemorative piece, but the principle remains that the judicious use of gold in your design and colour scheme will attract the eye to the salient points of the text and literally light up the colours.

"Gilding" is the application of gold as a highlight or as a major component of the design. The gold can be flat or applied over a base to achieve a relief effect which will catch the light even better.

For quick or inexpensive work, you can, of course, use gold paint which is available in bottles. It comes in various shades, ranging from greeny gold to a deep yellow colour, and is mostly powdered brass suspended in a volatile fluid.

Genuine gold is available in three different forms: powdered shell gold, so-called because it used to be sold in a half mussel shell; it is now available in small cakes which are used with water and a brush, exactly like watercolours. Shell gold gives a flat surface; the gold dries to a lustreless finish which can be polished to a high brilliance with an agate burnisher. Because shell gold is used like watercolour, it is good for small, highly intricate details or writing. It looks particularly good when used to highlight parts of an already painted decoration and sits well over deep-coloured gouaches.

Genuine gold is also available as gold leaf which can be applied to a raised gum base or size – gum ammoniac is recommended. Alternatively, gold leaf is applied to a gesso base which is a raised layer of plaster applied to paper or vellum with a pen or a brush. Gold leaf will produce a raised surface which is very shiny and catches the light in a way different from that of shell gold.

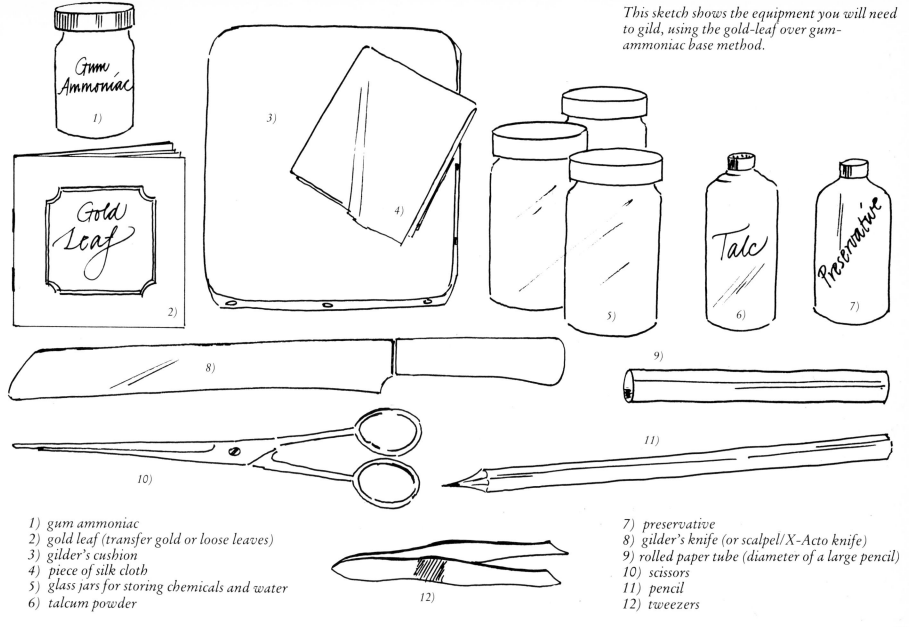

This sketch shows the equipment you will need to gild, using the gold-leaf over gum-ammoniac base method.

1) gum ammoniac
2) gold leaf (transfer gold or loose leaves)
3) gilder's cushion
4) piece of silk cloth
5) glass jars for storing chemicals and water
6) talcum powder

7) preservative
8) gilder's knife (or scalpel/X-Acto knife)
9) rolled paper tube (diameter of a large pencil)
10) scissors
11) pencil
12) tweezers

Alphabet. tiré de la Bible. du Roi Iean

Bibl. Nat. Franç. 15397.

Overleaf. *Alphabet and borders drawn from a fourteenth-century French bible. The initials are very ornate and show the white tracery typical of the period. An enlarged example of one of these letters is shown on page 119. The alphabet continues on page 79, 82 and 87.*

GILDING METHODS

Using shell gold. The gold tablet contains a water-soluble gum and should be used with distilled water applied with a brush. Once moistened, the gold can be applied with either a pen or a brush. You will have to experiment to see how much water you need to add, particularly when using a pen: too much water will result in a patchy, dull appearance; not enough and the pen will clog. To apply shell gold with a brush use only fine sable brushes and keep them for that purpose. Gold is very expensive and you will find that the distilled water you use will contain an amount of gold particles; save this water as you can eventually recycle the precious metal by letting the water evaporate. When you use shell gold for the background to a border, for instance, the gold can be applied before or after other painted decorations. But if you use it for delicate details, add those after the painting has been finished. Shell gold is easier to use than leaf gold and its liquid form makes it possible to use it very sparingly which may suit modern taste better than large panels of flat gilding. It is particularly effective when used as tiny dots over areas of intense colour, such as deep blues or vermilion, and some of the suggested pieces of work in this book (pages 114 and 141, for example) show how a delicate gold tracery can add to the colour balance.

After shell gold is fully dry, burnish it with an agate burnisher to raise the shine. The agate burnisher is a useful tool – the side is used to burnish and the point can be used to break and enrich the surface of a flat gold area. Medieval illuminators scored tiny patterns over gilded borders to great advantage. You will find numerous examples illustrated in this book.

Using the agate burnisher to polish shell gold.

Gilding with gold leaf. Gold leaf is available either as paper-backed "transfer gold" or as loose leaves separated by thin sheets of paper. Transfer gold is the easiest to use over a gum-ammoniac base and this is the method recommended for a beginner. Since the gold is attached to a backing, shapes can be drawn on and cut with an X-Acto knife or a scalpel and applied to the gum-ammoniac base. Gum ammoniac is also easier to prepare than gesso. In the early years of the nineteenth century it was frequently described in articles and books on illumination and was probably the most common technique used by the Victorians for gold-leaf application.

Gum ammoniac is obtained from a plant grown in Iran and North Africa. It should not be confused with gum arabic, however, which is used as a waterproofing agent in ink. Gum ammoniac is sold by artists' supply shops in the form of large crystals or globules and usually contains impurities which need to be removed.

Preparing gum ammoniac. Soak about 2 ounces (60 gm) of gum ammoniac in a jam jar. Add distilled water just to cover the gum. Leave to soak overnight. Strain the mixture through a fine sieve or cloth to get rid of the impurities. Pour the gum ammoniac into a clear jar that has a lid. You should add a little food dye or watercolour to make it easier to see when writing with it. One drop of chloroform or 2-naphthol will prevent it from becoming mouldy.

When you use the gum, it should be thick enough to leave the required raised line upon which to lay the gold leaf, but thin enough to flow easily from the quill. If you use a brush, wash it afterwards in warm water or in a solution of ammonia and water, otherwise it will set hard and the brush will be ruined.

Applying transfer gold to a gum base. For larger areas of gilding cut out your shapes carefully. To adhere to its base, the gold will need a certain amount of humidity. Using a paper tube, blow on the gum base, which will become sticky, and transfer the gold onto it. For small details or writing, simply press the gold down, using your fingers or a soft silk pad. It should stick without difficulty and to the gum base only. Do not press the gold down so hard as to disturb the gum base. If you find that gold has stuck only in patches, it probably means that not enough moisture was present: breathe on the gum again and apply more gold to cover the entire surface. Gold sticks to itself and you can add marginally to the shine of your illumination by laying two layers of gold instead of one. This method does not require burnishing and any excess gold can be removed with a soft brush kept for that purpose, or a silk

Blowing on the gum base to render it tacky enough to take the gold leaf.

pad. Any recalcitrant bits can be rubbed off the paper or vellum with a hard eraser (the kind that comes in pencil form for use with a typewriter is particularly useful for going around details).

With its slightly raised surface, gold leaf over gum ammoniac looks very attractive on a painted background. But one word of caution: paint tends to attract the gold leaf which will stick to it as well as on the gum base after you have breathed on it. To counteract this, dust a fine layer of talcum powder over the area before applying the gum base – just enough to absorb the moisture but not so much as to mix with the gum ammoniac and cause it to dry to a gritty consistency. For this reason, many people prefer to do the gilding first and then paint. As with everything in illumination, patience will be rewarded. Experiment until you feel confident and then try this technique on a piece of work, such as the initial R on page 107.

Using loose gold leaf. You can also use loose gold leaf over the gum-ammoniac base described above. The gold sheets come in a little book of finely beaten leaves about 2½ inches (65 mm) square. The best kind of gold leaf for illumination is 24 carat of pure unalloyed gold and "fine" gold which is 23¼ carat. Always hold the book by its spine with the gold leaves hanging down to avoid crumpling them into the spine. Any grease deposit will attract the gold, so any tool that will come in contact with it must be absolutely clean. Your fingers should never touch the gold. To cut the leaf, lay it on a pad of fine suede leather, or a proper gilder's cushion, if you have one. Cut the shapes required with a sharp knife with a straight blade. You can also cut shapes from the book itself, using sharp scissors and cutting both the gold leaf and the tissue paper interleaf. With tweezers you can then pick up your cut-out shapes and transfer them to the gum base, after breathing on it, as described earlier. It is relatively more difficult to handle the loose gold leaf than using transfer gold.

(Bibl. Nat. Lat. 7241).

Gold leaf over gesso. Gesso is a fine plaster that can be built up to a raised surface. This method of gilding appears to have been used in the late Middle Ages and will produce relief drawings which can be burnished to a sparkling finish. It is also the most difficult method of gilding and requires a lot of practice and patience, trial and error. Do not be put off trying, however; to quote Donald Jackson, the well-known calligrapher: "He who hesitates will not gild." We owe much to Jackson's work in recent years and to that of Graily Hewitt who, at the beginning of the century, experimented and rediscovered the techniques used by the illuminators of old.

Gesso has to be a thickish liquid which will nevertheless flow easily from a quill. It is drawn or lettered onto prepared vellum (page 35) and dries as a raised line on the surface that can be felt with the fingertip, rather like a scar or scab. The quill used for applying gesso has to be particularly flexible, with a longer than usual slit nib. For larger areas, you can use a brush. Building up the gesso layers will take considerable time to achieve the desired relief effect.

Preparing gesso. The following recipe is the one advocated by Donald Jackson; but as he himself points out, the "quantities are not sacrosanct." You will have to experiment and adjust the proportions to suit climate and your needs. Ambient humidity, always a crucial factor in illumination, plays a vital role when using gesso.

Ingredients:
2 parts raw brown sugar finely powdered or rock candy
16 parts slaked dental plaster
6 parts finely powdered titanium dioxide
1 part refined fish glue
Some colour (Armenian bole or any other red or yellow pigment that is not gritty)
Distilled water

Equipment:
6 in (150 mm) mortar and pestle
Rubber spatula
2 palette knives
Sheet of baking paper
Pinch of salt

Crush the sugar first to a fine powder. Wash out the mortar and mix the sugar with the other dry ingredients. Take a small quantity of the mixed ingredients and add enough distilled water to make a thick paste. Grind coarsely in the mortar then transfer the paste to another glass or ceramic container. Continue in this way until the whole of the dry ingredients have been converted into a coarse paste. Grind the paste again until all the gritty bits have disappeared (this could take thirty to forty minutes), adding distilled water to form a smooth, creamy paste. Use the spatula to scrape the paste from the sides of the mortar back to the bottom. This is a job that calls for patience and hard work, but the final results on the page will depend upon the careful grinding of the gesso base. When all the paste is absolutely smooth, scrape it off with a palette knife onto the baking paper to an even thickness. Wet the palette knife to ensure an even spreading of the paste.

Allow the gesso shape to dry in a dust-free atmosphere, but before the mass has entirely solidified, mark lines across it like toffee pieces to make it easier to break into convenient portions later on. Keep the dry gesso covered with a piece of cloth until you are ready to use it.

Although it is perfectly possible to use gesso before it hardens, experts like Donald Jackson maintain that better results are obtained if the gesso is first allowed to dry thoroughly and then tempered.

Bibl. Nat. Franc. 15397.

(Bibl. Nat. Franc. 13091).

Tempering gesso. To use gesso with a quill or a brush, it has to be thinned out with distilled water. First crush the gesso pieces into crumbs, and then add gradually the distilled water to form a mixture that will flow in a pen or a brush. Alternatively, you can use glair instead of water, as recommended by Donald Jackson (*see* glair recipe on page 60). Crumble the gesso sections as above into an egg cup, add a couple of drops of glair and allow the gesso to soak thoroughly for about ten minutes. Wearing a rubber glove, knead and press the mixture firmly to expel as much air as possible and avoid bubbles. Gradually, add more glair to reach the desired consistency. Try the mixture on your pen or brush until you are satisfied with the viscosity. Gesso can be used very thinly diluted and still produce the raised domed surface required for gilding. If air bubbles develop, prick them with a needle that has been slightly greased – by rubbing it between your fingertips, for instance. The gesso is now ready to use.

Applying gesso. If you have used gum sandarac to prime the writing surface of the vellum (*see* page 35), this should be removed from all areas where you intend to apply gesso. Burnish down the nap with an agate burnisher or the gesso may not "take." When working with gesso, the paper or vellum should be mounted flat, or the heavy wet gesso may run or sag. Using a pen, apply the gesso evenly, creating a domed, smooth line for the gold. Press the pen open to start the flow and ease it outwards to create the required shapes and continuous flawless lines. You will need to work fast to ensure that the gesso dries evenly. Mistakes are best rectified after the gesso has solidified. For larger surfaces, use a brush; this is a longer process, for you will have to build up the thickness of gesso, layer upon layer. Stir the gesso frequently, because the mixture tends to separate after a while.

Mistakes can be repaired and rough edges smoothed down when the gesso is fully dried. Scrape it carefully with a scalpel or X-Acto knife. It is better, however, to accept slight irregularities and undulations rather than end up with squared edges which will be difficult to burnish later.

Gilding over gesso. Humidity plays a large part in this process and the atmospheric conditions in your workroom on the day will influence your choice of method for applying gold leaf to your design. Whatever method you choose, have your burnisher, breathing tube, gilder's knife or scalpel and silk pad at the ready since speed of execution is important. Your work should be mounted on a smooth hard surface – marble, glass or even formica will be cool and will retain humidity. Cut out shapes of loose gold leaf as described on page 78.

In relatively humid conditions, you can burnish the gold through a piece of glassine paper, with or without breathing on the gesso. Burnish the gold after the gold has fused with the gesso. This method of indirect burnishing enables you to see the shape of the design clearly through the paper and makes it easier to tuck the edge of the gold leaf around the intricacies of the design. This is a good method for anyone inexperienced in using a burnisher. The gold can be polished afterwards, when the gesso is hard enough.

Another method is to press the gold leaf onto the gesso with a silk pad. The gold is burnished after the gesso has hardened, often without breathing on the gesso. This is a handy technique when ambient humidity is so high that some time would have to elapse between applying the gold and burnishing it.

In dry conditions, on the other hand, and provided you feel confident with the burnisher, you can apply the gold leaf directly with the burnisher. It is quick, but you need to be nimble, since the gesso may be very soft – in which case you should gently stroke the gold onto it with the burnisher. At other times a firmer pressure will be needed to ensure the proper adherence of the gold.

Coping with problems. If a portion of the design seems to repel the gold, even after breathing on it repeatedly, scrape the gesso with a sharp knife over a larger area than needed so as to even out the surface. This should create a key for the gold. Now breathe on it and apply gold leaf. Gold sticks to gold and it therefore does not matter if the edges of the gold leaf overlap. Check regularly that gesso has not stuck to the burnisher; if it has, remove it with a silk cloth or a tissue – never scrape it off.

There is not much you can do about ambient humidity, but the following points may be helpful. Increasing the sugar content in gesso will attract more dampness from the atmosphere, if necessary. In very dry conditions, a humidifier in the room will solve many problems. This is very effective, particularly in a small room. If the air is too damp, an electric heater will help. Avoid working under a strong overhead lamp which will dry your work; a cool strip-light placed above the work table is far better and more comfortable to work by.

If conditions are dry, resist the impulse to start gilding on freshly laid gesso; it may seem dry, but the paper or vellum underneath may still be wet.

Silver. Silver leaf or white gold will turn black within a short time when in contact with the air. To simulate silver, you can use aluminium or platinum leaf which will not tarnish. Aluminium is sold in small cakes, but is rather coarse. For fine work, use platinum leaf which is applied in the same way as gold leaf. The leaves are not as thinly beaten as gold, however, and this makes them a little more difficult to use.

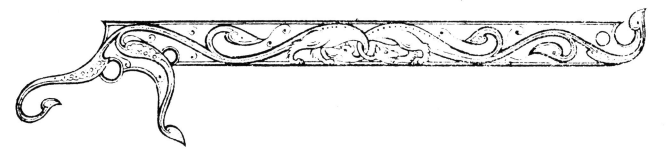

Keep a log of all your gilding experiments, both successes and failures. If at all possible, try to have a practical lesson in gilding from an experienced gilder or attend a demonstration. To quote Irene Base, one of the great practitioners of the art of gilding in the twentieth century: "Steady success in gilding can never be attained by a fixed rule, for the work does not behave in the same way twice, even on consecutive days under apparently exactly the same conditions. Success is most likely to come by flexibility in method, by resourcefulness in getting out of difficulties, and by a willingness to go back on special occasions to methods long discarded . . ."

This detail of a fourteenth-century border from a French manuscript has been enlarged to show the shading on the formalized foliage.

OUTLINING & FINISHING

In the nineteenth century, as in the Middle Ages, illuminators were concerned that colours by themselves would have a dull appearance and so they made use of additional outlines, fine white edging and hairline finishing. These additions heightened the effect of colours, gave an elaborate and brilliant feel to the work and, when used with restraint, created interesting, almost relief effects in the painting. Sometimes subjects were outlined in a deeper shade of the local colour – a pink flower might be outlined with crimson or a pale blue bow with darker blue. But in the *natural* treatment of the subject forming the illumination, everything was coloured and shaded as in nature. Ivory black or lamp black with a little gum water produced a fine and firm line, making it ideal for outlining as it retained its intense, glossy black appearance. With a little practice, the beginner would soon learn the best consistency to make it. As it evaporated, a few drops of water were added. For hairline finishing, using the same brush as for outlining, light lines upon a dark background would be added, and vice versa. White hairline finishing, unless used on a tiny scale, can overpower and spoil the effect of a design. The application of very fine lines requires delicate handling, and the exercise of considerable skill and patience. Fret-work, flowerlets, veins and dots were done in white on a dark ground with a free, firm touch. On some coloured grounds, however, it was necessary to go over the lines twice with the brush to ensure clarity because the white was absorbed into the colour underneath. Like everything else, practise makes perfect and looking at the examples that have been left by the masters of the past shows how these techniques can be used to best advantage.

For the geometrical diapers that were frequently used in backgrounds, the drawing-pen and small bow-pen were used. Sometimes a multitude of minute points of gold were placed over an entire area of dark background. Alternatively, large areas of gilding were indented with the point of the agate or a tracing-point to produce a glittering effect. Below are examples of geometrical patterning used in borders in colour but also often scored into gilded backgrounds.

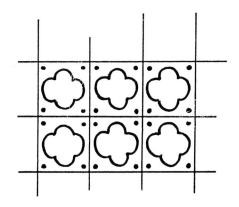

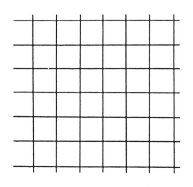

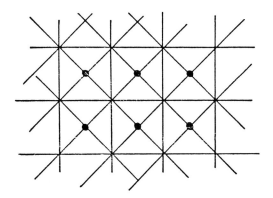

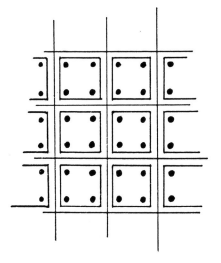

Overleaf. *Alphabet drawn from a fifteenth-century manuscript showing the growing taste for three-dimensional effects, achieved by the clever application of highlights. This alphabet is continued on pages 94 and 95.*

L'Alphabet est tiré d'un
manuscrit de la (Bibl. Nat.
Français 145)

Tous les fleurons de cette page
et les éléments de bordure de la
page suivante sont tirés des
heures illuminées (Latin 1173
Bibl. Nat.)

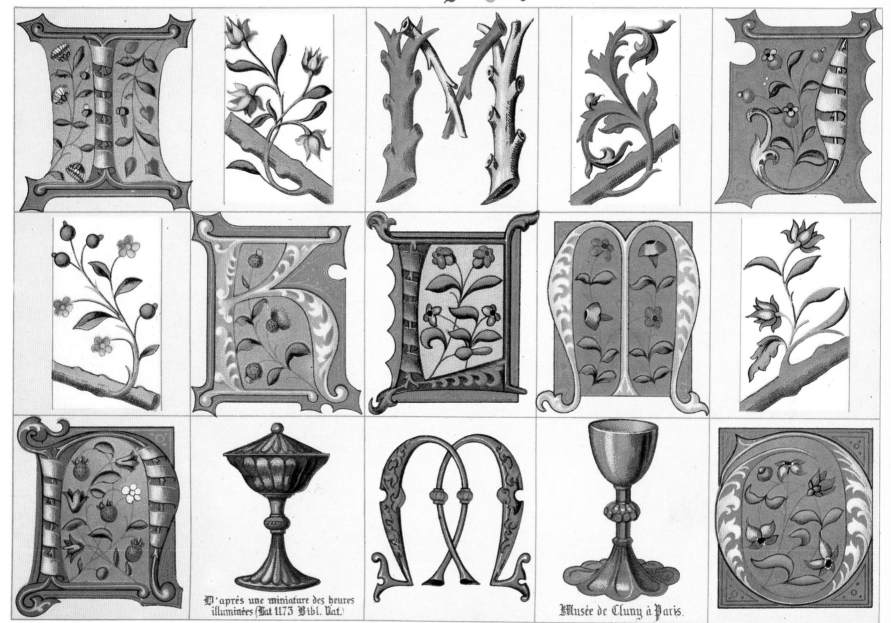

Documents du Moyen-Age XVᵉᵐᵉ siècle.

D'après une miniature des heures illuminées (Vat 1173 Bibl. Nat.)

Musée de Cluny à Paris.

Victorian illuminators, perhaps influenced by the popularity of black-and-white engraving, almost always preferred to outline. Used with discretion, black outlines make bright colours appear richer and increase their intensity. Their use is very much a question of personal taste. But moderation remains the key word. An excess of outlining, as of any other form of decoration, can easily "cheapen the effect," to quote Edward Johnston. Surrounding capital letters on a white or plain background, for instance, is rarely necessary:

On the other hand, outlining improves the appearance of letters on a busy or coloured background and provides, as Johnston adds, a "niche for the letter to rest in." Gold spots may be furred with black lines to emphasize their brightness:

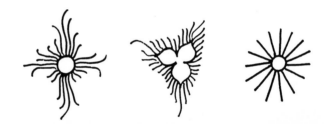

It is not easy to sum up the best approach to illuminating, but the following principles are those which have been adhered to by the most respected scribes both ancient and modern.

1) Choose a restricted range of pure bright pigments and make sure your work is clear and crisp.
2) Remember that spontaneity means knowing all the rules, but not being bound by them.
3) Plan your page and your book in order, and understand the underlying measurements, border proportions and text before you start writing.
4) Write the black-ink text first, leaving planned spaces for the illustrations and decorations.
5) Next write any coloured text or capital letters.
6) Carry out illumination and gold-leaf work.

But let Marcus Ward, illuminator to Queen Victoria, have the last word. In *Illuminating*, he wrote:

"We must, however, caution our readers against supposing that excellence in the art of illumination is to be reached by mechanical helps, or even by attention to the best written rules, without careful study and persevering practice. Above all, there should be that innate perception of the beautiful and the graceful, both in nature and art, without which study and perseverance will fail in their effect. In the art of Design, more especially, excellence cannot be attained otherwise than by long continued application directed by good taste."

1

2

3

4

Bordure d'un manuscrit de la
(Bibl. Nat. Franc. 54)

1. 2. 3. 4. Détails de Bordures des
heures de M. D. Lafin 1166. (Bibl. Nat.)

1

Tiré du frontispice du Livre des
Tournois (Franç. 2692 Bibl. Nat.)

2

3

4

5

1.2.3. Détails de Bordures du Manuscrit
(Franç. 54 Bibl. Nat.)

4.5. Extraits d'une miniature des
heures illuminées (Lat. 1173 Bibl. Nat.)

A detail from a fifteenth-century manuscript.

PLANNING THE WORK

Looking through the beautiful illustrations collected by Guillot from old manuscripts, one is struck by the recurrence of motifs from the natural world. Portrayed realistically, as well as in more stylized and formalized versions, rabbits, cats and sheep as well as birds and butterflies; flowers, foliage and fruit run round the pages so carefully planned by the medieval artists. Such mythical beasts as griffons, dragons and feathered serpents also convolute in the borders or lend their shapes to initial letters.

The human form is also a commonly used motif. Earlier manuscripts portrayed peasant couples, farmers and clerics, kings and queens as well as saints, angels and the Virgin Mary.

Not infrequently, the illuminator added humorous touches to his work, showing his delight with his subject.

There is much that can be learned from looking at old manuscripts and at the way medieval illuminators designed and planned their work. They were motivated by religious faith and the desire to enhance the text they worked on: the decorations they introduced were rarely gratuitous. This is a good principle to keep in mind when planning your own piece of work. You may be designing an elaborate border around a favourite poem to be framed and hung on the wall. Like the medieval artist, you will be focusing the reader's eye on the salient points of the text and sharing with him or her your own delight in the poet's words which you will have spent a long time lettering. You should therefore always have a good reason for introducing any detail in the design. There should be a general purpose and a meaning in every detail. Consider first what idea is to be conveyed, and, second, how to convey it. Then the design will acquire a unity and completeness which will be lacking in a design worked out at random, or only because it looks pretty.

Designing initials. The first consideration is legibility. However elaborately an initial may be decorated, it must be read at first glance. The legibility of coloured letters is best ensured by keeping to a decided and prominent colour for the body of the letter, which should contrast strongly with the colours of the ornamentation. The fillings of initials are endless in their variety; good outlines may express the vigour of the drawing, and the elegance and harmony of the design, but to acquire a thorough understanding of the delicacy of finish of details and the charm of well-developed colours in illuminating, there is no substitute for looking at the work of the great illuminators of the past and also at the pieces produced by present-day artists (*see* list of places to visit on page 136.

The success of a piece of calligraphy, and even more of illumination, depends on careful planning of the whole work. The choice of painted decorations and gilding should harmonize with the lettering used for the text. If you are planning a piece of work based on the many medieval examples reproduced in this book, the Lombardic alphabet or the Church Text reproduced on pages 24 and 25 would look well with them. On the other hand, if you are copying the Victorian design on page 129 for a gift as a commemoration of a happy occasion, for example, you may wish to use a more casual, lighter script.

Careful planning is even more vital if you are working on a whole book rather than on an isolated piece of work. After the plan has been decided on, make a rough sketch; in the case of a book, prepare a dummy. In this way, you will know exactly what comes on which page and you will avoid discovering too late that a full-page illumination falls on the "flesh" or smooth side of the vellum (*see* page 32). If you are working on paper rather than vellum, this problem will not present itself, but you will still have to know whether an illustration falls on the right- or the left-hand page (*see* rules for page design page 108) and that you have left yourself enough space at the bottom of a piece of text for a planned decorated finial. This preparation work may take days, but it will be worthwhile.

While you are planning your work, using elements traced out of this book or working out your own drawings, you will find it helpful to trace them roughly on tracing paper and arrange them together on the page, moving them about, adjusting the size of the various elements in relation to each other until you reach the desired

composition. You may be impatient to start painting and illuminating, but careful planning will save you the frustration of having to discard a page on which you have already spent many hours lettering the text. Again, by working on tracing paper, you can try out variations and different ideas before actually transferring them to the paper or vellum. Mistakes are difficult to rectify on vellum and it is better to wait until you are absolutely sure of your composition.

PLANNING THE WORK

Preparing the work. Place the piece of paper or vellum you want to draw on onto the drawing board. Attach into place with drawing pins. Remember that the sheet should always be larger than the final page/piece of work. To prevent the margins from being soiled, attach a sheet of thin card as a mask with a flap the size of the page cut in it over the paper/prepared vellum.

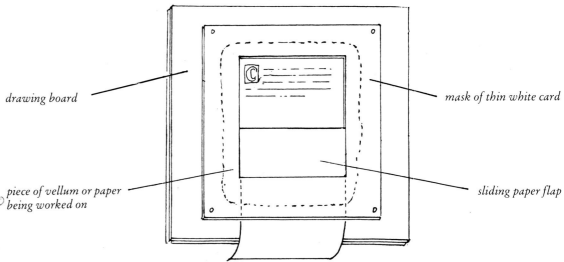

drawing board

mask of thin white card

piece of vellum or paper being worked on

sliding paper flap

By partly sliding back the flap, you can protect the sections you are not actually working on from smudging and accidental spills.

Drawing the outline. Start by making a careful transfer of the outline, using a hard pencil which will give a clear, clean line that will not smudge. Rub a soft (2B) pencil on the reverse of the tracing paper. Position your transfer over the page of paper or vellum you are working on and fix it with masking tape in such a way as to enable you to lift a corner from time to time and check that the design is being transferred accurately, but without disturbing the register. Go over the design with a hard pencil, making sure the whole pattern has been transferred. The drawing should appear clearly but not so dark as to show in the finished work.

This is a practice exercise, but when you reach the stage of producing your own designs you may wish to transfer the main outlines of the drawings, putting in the details freehand. This will depend on your confidence as a draughtsman. It is difficult to remove pencil lines from vellum, in particular; the black lead fusing with the animal matter of the skin can never be properly erased. India rubber or bread often leave a greasy smudge and pumice powder tends to pull up the surface of the vellum, thus attracting dust and dirt in future handling.

When you are absolutely happy with the drawing, you can either keep it in pencil as it is or go over it with a fine pen or brush loaded with a pale shade of watercolour or with diluted ink (waterproof ink with distilled water). When it is dry, you can rub off any remaining pencil mark with a soft rubber, ensuring that the pencil does not smudge across your work. Remember, however, that it will be very difficult to get rid of the watercolour or inked outline if you decide to change a section of the drawing later.

At this stage, letter the text. Cover it with a piece of card when it is finished to prevent it from being stained while you paint.

Gilding. If you use shell gold for the background (*see* page 76), it can be applied either before or after painting the floral motif. If you wish to burnish the shell gold, it may be better to gild and burnish before painting or take extra care not to disturb the paint, if burnishing at a later stage. If you use transfer gold over a gum-ammoniac base (*see* page 77), you should gild the background first as paint tends to attract gold

Above. *Left- and right-hand pages with elaborately gilded and painted margins.*

Opposite. *Initial letters copied from a fourteenth-century manuscript composed and written for Robert, King of Naples, who succeeded to the throne in 1309.*

Colouring the design. Mix your colours with care and begin by applying the lighter colours, gradually working to the darkest. Add any black outlines, if desired, using a fine pen. Finally, add highlights to your painting using a very fine brush.

The gold background in this border has been scored with tiny dots, using the point of the agate burnisher. Practise on a trial piece first, or the entire picture could be spoiled if this is not done with the required lightness of touch.

Page layout. For most calligraphers, but particularly for anyone who wants to embark on bookwork, it is important to know how to design a page. In the thirteenth century Villard de Honnecourt, an architect from Picardy in France, devised an ingenious method of finding the so-called "golden rule," the optimum proportions for margins, text area and decorations on a book page. This method is applicable to any page size. The sketch below shows how it works:

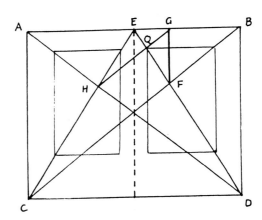

1) Draw the long diagonals AD, CB.
2) Draw short diagonals CE, DE.
3) Draw the vertical FG.
4) Draw the line GH.
5) You now have the vital point Q. Draw horizontal lines to cut CB and vertical lines to cut ED to get perfect text margins.

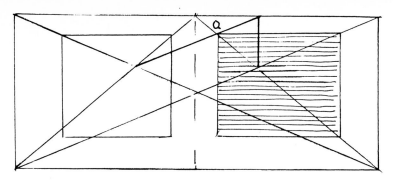
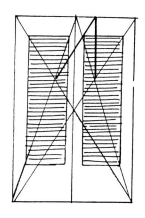

Examples of different book shapes and the text and margins layouts which evolve by using the "golden rule."

As a result of his research into the methods of work of medieval illuminators, Edward Johnston established the following formulae for well-proportioned pages, ready for illumination and lettering:

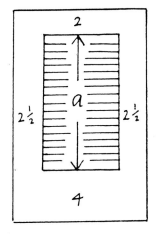

A single sheet

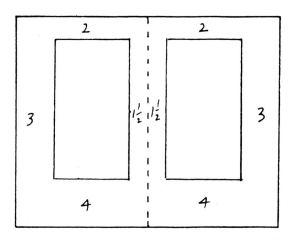

A double-page spread

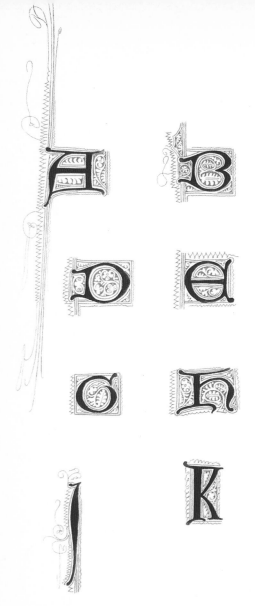

*Letters copied from a large folio
Gradual or Antiphony, English, c 1400.*

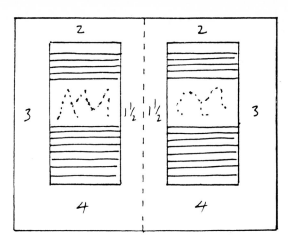

Here is a double-page spread for a book with spaces left for illustrations a little over half-way up the page. Although this can be judged by eye, work out exactly where your lines of text begin and end, then allocate space for illustrations.

If a book is to be bound, remember to allow extra space in the spine (gutter margin) to allow for the stitching. The binder may wish to trim the pages after binding and you should also add a minimum of ¼ inch (5 mm) around the other margins to allow for this.

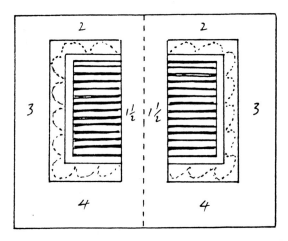

This is a typical layout for an illuminated double-page spread, allowing for borders on three sides of the block of text. When considering a layout, always look upon the double-page spread as an entity. The two pages may be different in their decoration, of course, but they should always harmonize with each other.

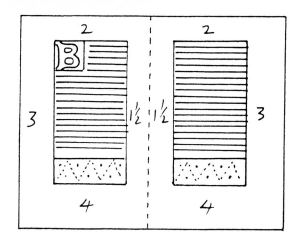

This layout incorporates a decorated initial, text and decorative borders at the foot of the page.

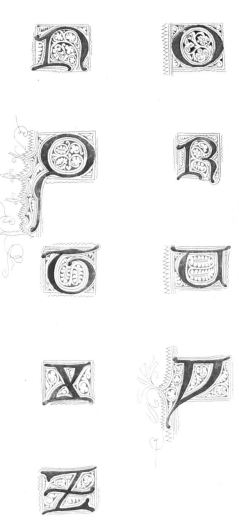

In the same way as you must carefully work out the elements of illustration and gilding, so must your text be carefully planned. Always rule lines on which to position the text. These can be lightly pencilled in. These lines should be *just* visible, otherwise you may damage the surface of the paper and soil the vellum, if you have to erase them after the lettering is completed. The medieval illuminators would prick through several layers of parchment to ensure that the text would "back," that means that the lines of calligraphy would fall at exactly the same spot on both sides of the page on every page throughout the book (*see* page 39). Look carefully at medieval manuscripts: the discreet ruling out of the text is frequently still visible, but it is so faint that it does not mar the beauty of the work.

PROJECTS & POSSIBILITIES

This section is intended to serve as a resource and an inspiration. Included here is a number of alphabets that are suitable for illumination or for calligraphy used in conjunction with illumination. There are black and white outlines for a variety of borders, with suggestions for their illumination. These can be traced as they are, or enlarged, or adapted to suit a particular piece of work. In addition, there are step-by-step instructions for illuminating and colouring a letter and some unusual heraldic designs.

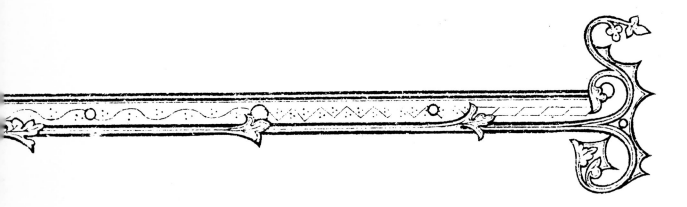

Opposite. *Two left-hand page outlines to trace and colour. The guidelines for the text should be just visible.*

105

This initial letter combines the use of gold leaf over a gum ammoniac base for the background and shell gold for the decoration over the coloured initial.

Initial drawn from a fifteenth-century manuscript and enlarged.

On the right is the basic outline, drawn large to show the details. Trace it and transfer it onto a piece of good-quality paper by rubbing a soft pencil over the back of the tracing and then going over the tracing itself with a hard pencil. Redraw the pencil outline with diluted ink (waterproof ink and distilled water); rub off any remaining pencil marks.

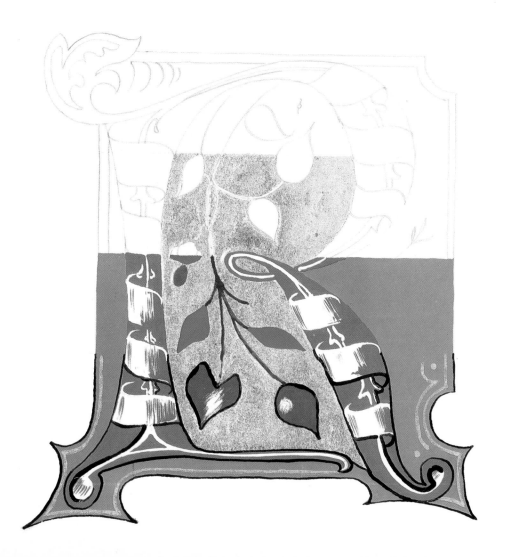

Illuminating and colouring a letter

1) Apply the gum ammoniac as explained on page 85; blow on it through the paper tube. Holding the transfer gold by its paper backing, press the leaf on the gum base as soon as it is sticky. You can apply more than one layer of gold as it will stick to itself. Any particle of gold that may have stuck to the paper can be removed with a soft brush or a piece of silk.

2) Apply the colours starting with the blue, then the pink, dark red and green and finally the white highlights which should be applied with a fine brush. Use gouache paints which dry to a fine opaque finish.

3) Draw the black outlines with ink using a mapping pen.

4) Add the shell-gold edging with a brush. Use a pen if you want really fine lines of consistent thickness.

Enlarging and transferring a drawing. This drawing can easily be traced and, like all the outlines in this book, and indeed all the illustrations, can be enlarged to suit your own requirements.

To enlarge a drawing, first square up a piece of tracing paper into ½-inch (1-cm) squares. If the artwork is complex, make the squares even smaller. Place this grid over the picture, or a clear photocopy, and trace the drawing as shown.

Place another piece of transparent paper over this tracing and draw a diagonal line from the bottom left-hand corner of the picture to the top right-hand corner and extend it to the required height for the enlarged drawing. Using this diagonal as a guide, and keeping the same left and bottom lines, mark the four corners of the new size on the second piece of tracing paper and square it up into the same number of squares as there are on your original tracing. Copy the design, square by square, onto the new

grid. The enlarged drawing can then be transferred onto paper or vellum by rubbing a soft pencil at the back of the transfer and then going over all the lines with a hard pencil.

If you have access to a photocopying machine that enlarges by a range of percentages, the task of enlarging a drawing is greatly facilitated. Simply make a tracing of the enlarged photocopy and transfer it onto paper or vellum as described.

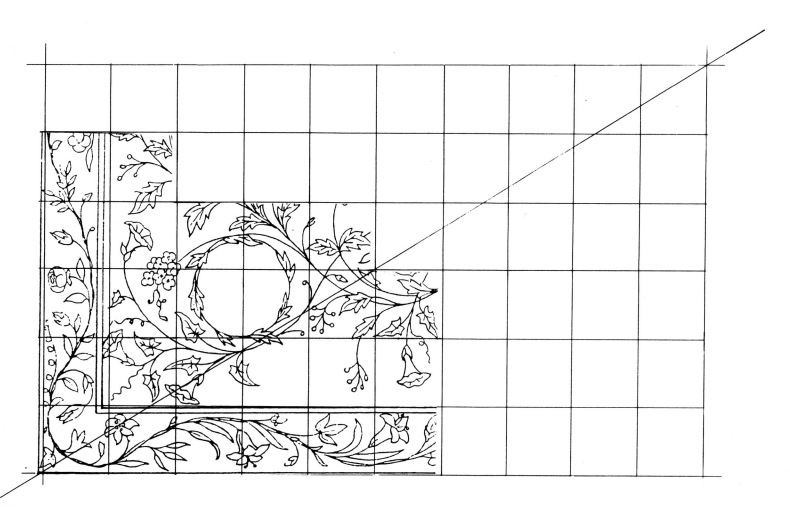

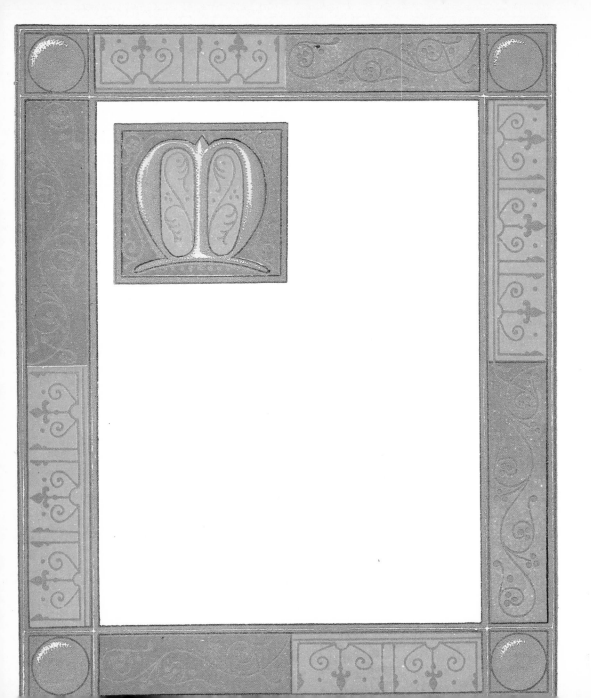

A border from a thirteenth-century French bible. The rectangular frame may be measured and drawn with a ruler. The golden tendrils can be traced off or drawn freehand. Use the raised gold-leaf over gum-ammoniac method for the large areas of gilding and pick out the filigree decorations in shell gold after the painting has been completed. This treatment would emphasize the difference in luminosity produced by both types of gilding.

This is a simple twelfth-century border in Romanesque style. It would make a handsome frame for a short poem or a proverb.

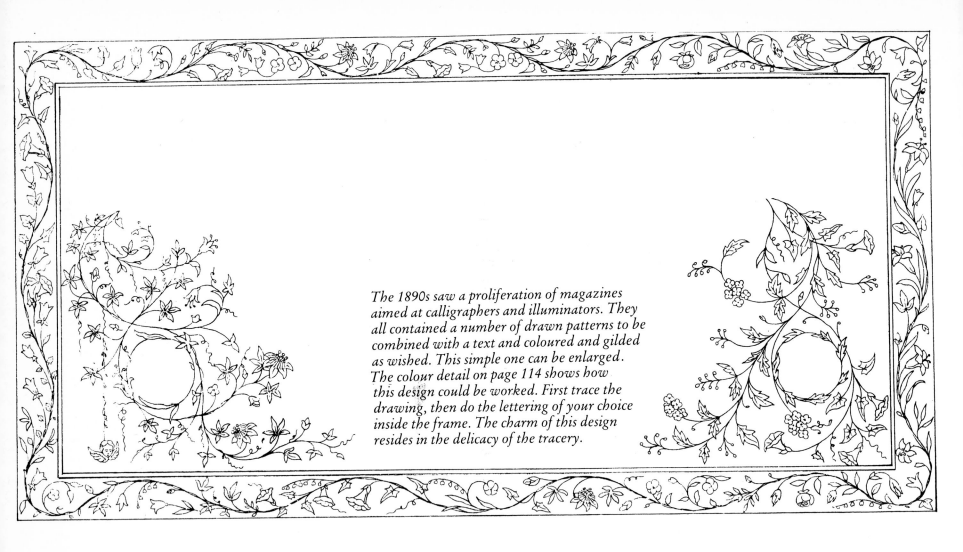

The 1890s saw a proliferation of magazines aimed at calligraphers and illuminators. They all contained a number of drawn patterns to be combined with a text and coloured and gilded as wished. This simple one can be enlarged. The colour detail on page 114 shows how this design could be worked. First trace the drawing, then do the lettering of your choice inside the frame. The charm of this design resides in the delicacy of the tracery.

A coloured detail of the border on the right is reproduced on page 115.

112

Right. *Small touches of gilding set off the design; and the only colour used was Ultramarine mixed with a dab of Permanent White. The method used here is transfer gold over a gum-ammoniac base. Gilding should be done after the calligraphy of the text is complete but before applying the colour. Gouache was used for the colour as it is opaque. It can be applied with a pen or a fine brush. If you do not want to gild, use a second colour instead of the gold.*

Left. *This cartouche is copied from a marble tomb in Rouen Cathedral in France (sixteenth century).*

This delicate design has no gilding. Gouache was used, but with a watery brush, except for the solid lines at the edges of the border and the formal pattern that holds the design together. The dry brush technique was used to pick out the details at the centres of the flowers. The colours used were: Burnt Sienna, Van Dyke Brown, Naples Yellow and Cadmium Lt. Green.

Initial letter drawn from a sixteenth-century French manuscript and enlarged to show the details.

There is a coloured detail of this border on page 118.

There is a suggested colour treatment for this cartouche on page 119.

A B C D E F G H I J K L M
N O P Q R S T V W X Y
Z ❖ ANNO · DOMINI ❖

Above. *Initials drawn by Henry Shaw for his book on medieval alphabets, published in 1845. They originate from brasses in Lübeck Cathedral in Germany.*

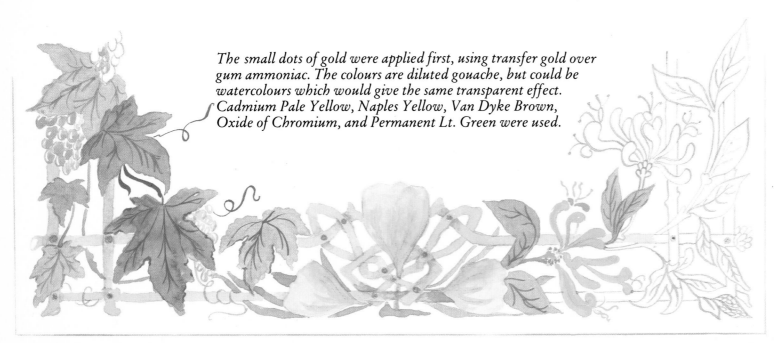

The small dots of gold were applied first, using transfer gold over gum ammoniac. The colours are diluted gouache, but could be watercolours which would give the same transparent effect. Cadmium Pale Yellow, Naples Yellow, Van Dyke Brown, Oxide of Chromium, and Permanent Lt. Green were used.

Enlarged initial drawn from a fourteenth-century French bible. It shows, in particular, the beautiful effect of hairline white finishing drawn over the flat-painted body of the initial. The letter is highly decorated on a gilded and painted background, which is also picked out with white hairline finishes, and yet the letter is immediately legible – a tribute to the skill of the artist.

Gilding was not used for this cartouche, which was done in gouache. The colours are Bengal Rose with white, Permanent Lt. Green and Oxide de Chromium (green).

This border is designed for an upright left-hand page, but could easily be adapted to form a frame with borders of equal width. It is shown in colour on page 122.

This page outline is another example of a dense drawing that at first appears highly complex but less so when you have identified the main curves that act as a framework to the design. The flowing lines of the vine start at the bottom left-hand corner and convolute around the text area in a profusion of leaves and tendrils. Look at the illustrations on pages 86 and 87 for possible treatment for this page.

121

The outline for this handsome design for an
upright left-hand page with its floral margins
is shown on page 120. The gilded background,
which should be applied first after completing
the lettering on the page, has been scored with
tiny dots.

This enlarged detail taken from a thirteenth-century bible, of a dog and a hare looking up expectantly at a fig tree, shows the medieval artist's delight in portraying the natural world. The subjects stand against a solid gilded background, but for a lighter effect you could instead use a blue wash speckled with tiny gold dots. Shell gold would work well for this purpose.

A suggested colour treatment for this design is shown on page 126.

This heraldic design would look well painted in warm tones, using gouache. Heraldry, by tradition, calls for pure and bright colours. Black and white are also much used. Gilding is common for shields, but as the details are intricate you will find it easier and more satisfying to use simulated gold (gold paint) rather than shell gold or gold leaf, unless you are an experienced gilder. Instead of gold you could use a brilliant yellow or an ochre. Silver is usually left white. If you are doing a heraldic design which will be printed by a four-colour process, remember to use gold paint instead of shell gold or raised gold leaf which are difficult to reproduce.

On page 127 there are examples of heraldic details.

The gilding of this simple but effective border
is restricted to the centre of each motif
and is just sufficient to catch the light and
enrich the design. Start with the gold, as usual,
if you are using the gold-leaf over gum-
ammoniac method (see gilding section); if you
prefer to use shell gold, it should also be put in
first as you may damage the paint when
burnishing. Working with gouache, Ethna
Gallacher then applied the pink (a mixture of
Bengal Rose with a touch of Permanent
White) and finished off with the blue
(Ultramarine and white).

The sketch on the left shows the simplicity of the framework for most of the designs collected
by Ernest Guillot. If you want to adapt or copy any of them, try finding out their "bare
bones" by making a very rough tracing of the main pattern first. You can then draw the
details freehand or trace them. The daisy pattern is copied from a frieze on a chimney piece at
the Château d'Ecouen in France (sixteenth century).

Some fine heraldic details drawn by Henry Shaw from manuscripts in the British Museum.

A coloured detail of this drawing appears on page 130.

This is an unusual design for a special message. A coloured detail is reproduced on page 130.

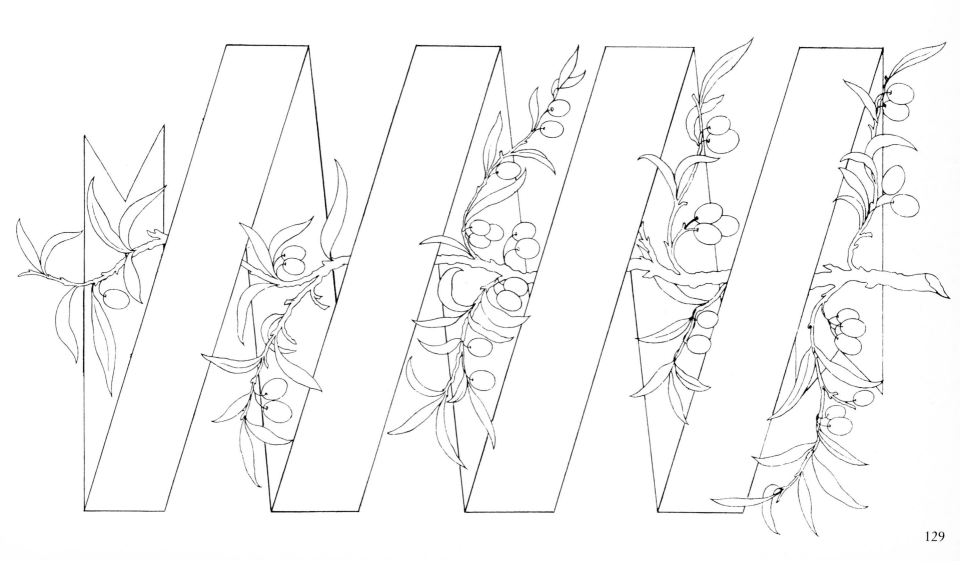

129

Below. *Coloured detail of the pattern shown on the previous page. The colours used are Permanent Lt. Green, Oxide of Chromium and Alizarin Crimson.*

and a Happy New Year

Left. *The colours used are Permanent Lt. Green, Cadmium Pale Yellow, Bengal Rose, Alizarin Crimson, Van Dyke Brown with a touch of Bengal Rose. Gouache was used but with a watery brush to create a watercolour, transparent effect.*

130

For this design, the centre of the motifs has been picked out in gold using the gold-leaf over gum-ammoniac technique. Apply the details in Cadmium Pale Yellow and complete by filling in the green motifs using Permanent Lt. Green with a touch of Oxide of Chromium.

These Lombardic-style capitals are particularly suitable for gilding. Their opulent shapes lend themselves well to the gum-ammoniac and gold-leaf process. Use these letters sparingly as initials.

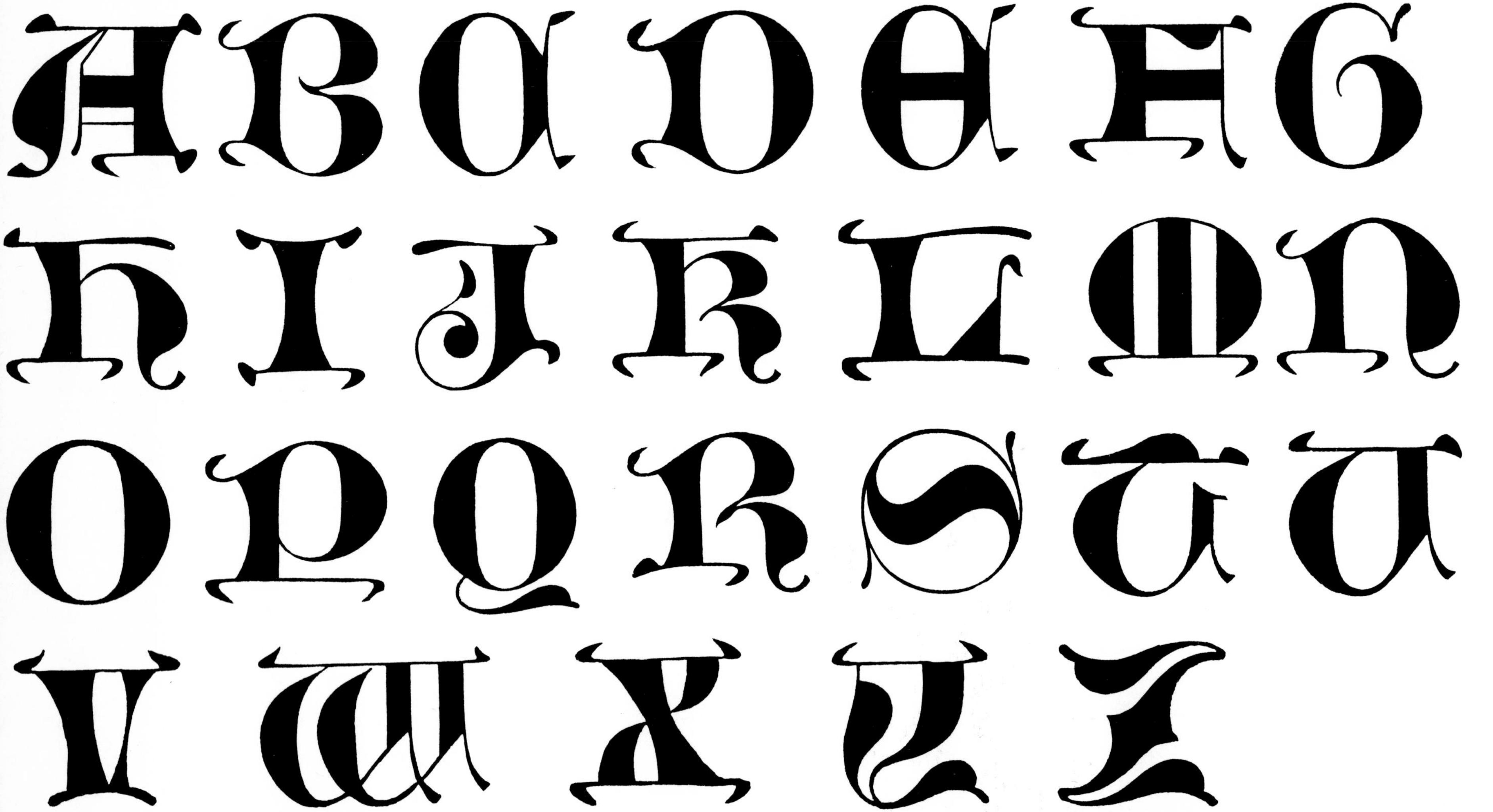

ABCDEFG

HIJKLMN

OPQRSTU

VWXYZ

132

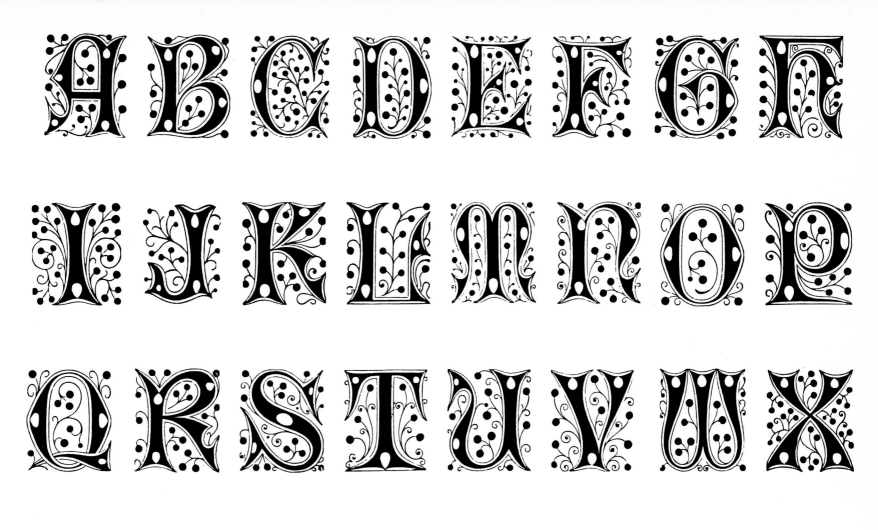

These Victorian letters are very suitable for gilding. They are best used singly, as initials, for they are too ornate for forming complete words.

133

SUGGESTED READING

Angel, Marie — *The Art of Calligraphy*, Robert Hale and Scribner's, 1978

Angel, Marie — *Painting for Calligraphers*, Pelham Books and Overlook Press, 1984

Anon — *The Arte of Limming*, 1573; reprinted facsimile by the Society of Scribes and Illuminators, 1979

Avi-Yonah, Michael — *Ancient Scrolls*, Cassell, 1973

Backhouse, Janet — *The Illuminated Manuscript*, Phaidon, Oxford, 1976

Camp, Ann — *Pen Lettering*, A & C Black, 1984

Cennini, d'Andrea Cennino — *Il Libro dell'Arte*, c1390; trans D.V. Thompson, Dover, 1954

Child, Heather Ed. — *The Calligrapher's Handbook*, (new edition) A & C Black and Pentalic, 1985

Child, Heather; Collins, Heather; Hechle, Ann; Jackson, Donald — *More Than Fine Writing: Irene Wellington: Calligrapher (1904-84)*, Pelham Books and Overlook Press, 1986

Diringer, David — *The Alphabet*, Vols I and II, revised Hutchinson, 1968

Gaur, Albertine — *A History of Writing*, The British Library, 1984

Harthan, J. — *Books of Hours*, Thames & Hudson, 1977

Hewitt, W. G. — *Lettering for Students and Craftsmen*, Seeley Service, 1930

Jackson, Donald — *The Story of Writing*, Studio Vista, 1981

Johnston, Edward — *Writing & Illuminating & Lettering*, John Hogg, 1906; reissued A & C Black and Taplinger, 1983

Jones, Owen — *The Grammar of Ornament*, Day & Son, 1850; reprinted Omega Books, 1986

*Laurie, A. P. — *The Painter's Methods and Materials*, Seeley Service, 1926

Mahoney, Dorothy — *The Craft of Calligraphy*, Pelham Books and Pentalic, 1981

*Ogg, Oscar — *The 26 Letters*, Harrap, 1949

Osley, A. S. Ed. — *Calligraphy and Palaeography*, Faber & Faber, 1965

Osley, A. S. — *Scribes and Sources*, Faber & Faber, 1980

Pacht, Otto — *Book Illumination in the Middle Ages*, O.U.P. and Harvey Miller, 1984

†Shaw, Henry — *Illuminated Ornaments from MSS of the Middle Ages*, Wm. Pickering, 1833

†Shaw, Henry — *Alphabets Numerals and Devices of the Middle Ages*, Wm. Pickering, 1845

Thompson, D.V. — *Materials of Medieval Painting*, Allen & Unwin, 1936

Tymms W. and Wyatt D. — *The Art of Illuminating*, Day & Sons, 1860; reprinted Wordsworth Editions, 1987

Valentine, L. N. — *Ornament in Medieval Manuscripts*, Faber & Faber, 1965

Whalley, Joyce — *Writing Instruments and Accessories*, David & Charles, 1975

*Available from public libraries by request
†Available at the British Museum Library

Right. *Miniature reproduced from a fourteenth-century French bible. The two shades of red used in the background give a feel of opulence to the piece.*

Reproduction d'une miniature de la Bible du Roi Jean. (Bibl. Nat. Franc. 15397)

GUIDE TO VIEWING ILLUMINATED BOOKS & MANUSCRIPTS

Most manuscripts are so valuable and insured for so much money that getting to see the originals except for a few in glass cases is not easy. Manuscripts tend to be locked away in the dark for preservation, and photography with lights or flash is seldom permitted. Always try, therefore, to see items on public display and look out for special exhibitions. Fees for access to certain manuscripts are often very high and sometimes only one or two interested scholars are allowed in at a time.

Therefore, to avoid disappointment if you wish to visit any of the sources listed below, it is essential to write or telephone for an appointment in advance. You are unlikely to see any beautiful manuscripts by just going to a museum, college or library without prior notice.

To gain some idea of what manuscripts each museum contains, it is possible to write and ask for a list. These lists usually contain many thousands of items, so you will need to inform them of your special area of interest. There is usually a small charge for this service.

France
Archives Nationales
60 rue des Francs-Bourgeois
75141 Paris CEDEX 03

Bibliothèque Municipale
13 Avenue de Champagne
51200 Epernay

Austria
Kunsthistorisches Museum
Burgring 5
A-1010 Wien 1

Germany
Staatsbibliothek Bamberg
Neue Residenz
Domplatz 8
86 Bamberg

Staatsbibliothek Preussischer
Kulturbesitz
Postfach 1407
1000 Berlin 30

Bayerische Staatsbibliothek Museum
Postfach 1500
D-8000 Munchen 34

Universitatsbibliothek Munchen
Geschwister – Scholl, Platz 1
8000 Munchen 22

Ireland
Trinity College Library
University of Dublin
College Street
Dublin 2

Italy
Biblioteca Medicea-Laurenziana
Piazza S. Lorenzo 9
Firenze

Biblioteca Apostolica Vaticana
Vatican City

Biblioteca Capitolare
Piazza Duomo 13
37100 Verona

United Kingdom
Craft Study Centre
Holburne Museum
1 Great Pulteney Street
Bath BA24 4DB

Magdalene College
Cambridge CB3 0AG

Trinity College Library
Cambridge CB2 1TZ

The Dean and Chapter Library
The College
Durham DH1 3EH

The British Museum
Department of Manuscripts
Great Russell Street
London, WC1B 3DG

The Victoria and Albert Museum Library
Cromwell Road
London SW7 2RL

The Bodleian Library
Department of Western Manuscripts
Oxford OX2 3BG

United States
The Walters Art Gallery
Baltimore, Md. 21201

Graphic Conservation Department
R.R. Donnelley & Sons, Inc.
223 Martin Luther King Drive
Chicago, III, 60616

Minnesota Manuscript Initiative
University of Minnesota
Minneapolis, Minnesota

The Pierpont Morgan Library
29 East 36th Street,
New York, NY 10016

The Huntington Library
Manuscripts Department
San Marino, California 91108

Overleaf. *A typical sixteenth-century style of letters. The art of the illuminator was changing: these initials are hardly calligraphic, in that they cannot be pen-formed, but are drawn and painted and stylized. In effect, they are becoming more decorative than functional. This alphabet is continued on pages 142 and 143.*

Pour rester fidèles au caractère polychrome de notre collection nous avons interprété en couleurs les éléments empruntés à la sculpture aux estampes et aux imprimés; la nature de l'original est d'ailleurs rappelée par la mention qui accompagne chaque document.

Cartouche tiré du tombeau de Louis de Brézé. Cathédrale de Rouen. (marbre)

Alphabet composé d'après des documents du Château de Blois.

Frise de la cheminée du Château d'Ecouen. (pierre)

III

I

IIII

II

1.2.3. Fragments de pilastres du
jubé de la Cath. de Limoges. (pierre)

4. Tiré d'un manuscrit
N° 10563. (Bibl. nat.)

139

LIST OF SUPPLIERS

United Kingdom

Winsor & Newton Ltd
51 Rathbone Place
London W1P 1AB

George Rowney & Co Ltd
12 Percy Street
London W1A 2BP

Reeves/Dryad
178 Kensington High Street
London W8 7NX

Falkiner Fine Papers
76 Southampton Row
London WC1B 4AR

Wiggins Teape Paperpoint
130 Long Acre
London WC2E 9AL
    and
26 Calthorpe Road
Edgbaston
Birmingham B15 1RP

William Cowley Parchment Works
97 Caldecote Street
Newport Pagnell, Bucks M16 0DB

George M. Whiley Ltd
Firth Road
Houstoun Industrial Estate
Livingston
West Lothian EH54 5DJ

Materials available

nibs, non-waterproof inks,
penholders and brushes

nibs, non-waterproof inks,
penholders and brushes

nibs, non-waterproof inks,
penholders and brushes

fine papers and all gilding
materials

fine papers

parchment and vellum

gold leaf

William Wright & Sons Ltd
Grove Avenue
Lymm
Cheshire WA13 0HG

gold leaf

W. Habberley Meadows Ltd
5 Saxon Way
Chelmsley Wood
Birmingham B37 5AY

gold leaf

Stonehouse & Sons
Unit 1, Grove Avenue
Lymm
Cheshire WA13 0HF

gold leaf

Buck & Ryan
101 Tottenham Court Road
London W1P 0DY

sharpening stones and knives

Philip Poole
181 Drury Lane
London WC2B 5QL

most calligraphic materials,
gilding, pigments

Cornelissen
105 Gt Russell St
London WC2

most calligraphic materials,
gilding, pigments

Duchy Gilding Co
(Mail Order Co)
The Old Mortuary Studio
Gylling Street
Falmouth, Cornwall

gilding, quills

United States

Arthur Brown
2 West 46th Street
New York, N.Y. 10036

Calpen
176 Jaxine Dr. Altadena
California 91001

Charrette Corporation
2000 Massachusetts Avenue
Cambridge, Massachusetts 02140

Carl Heinrich Company
711 Concord Avenue
Cambridge, Massachusetts 02138

B. L. Makepeace, Inc
1266 Boylston Street
Boston, Massachusetts 02215

Pentalic Corporation
132 West 22nd Street
New York, N.Y. 10011

Joseph Torch Inc
29 West 15th Street
New York, N.Y.

Werco
2340 West Nelson Street
Chicago
Illinois 60618

Materials available

pens, inks, gold leaf
and powdered gold

professionally prepared quills and reeds

fine papers, pens

fine papers, pens

fine papers, pens

pumice (pounce), gum sandarac,
vellum, gold leaf and all
supplies for gold work

fine hand-made papers,
pens and nibs

calfskin parchment
available, although mostly
manufactured for use on
drums and as lampshades

Détail du Jubé
de la Cathédrale de Limoges (pierre)

II

III

1. Ecusson du tombeau
de Valentine Balbiani.
provenant de l'église Ste Catherine du Val

I

2 et 3. Détails tirés
de la Cathédrale d'Evreux (bois)

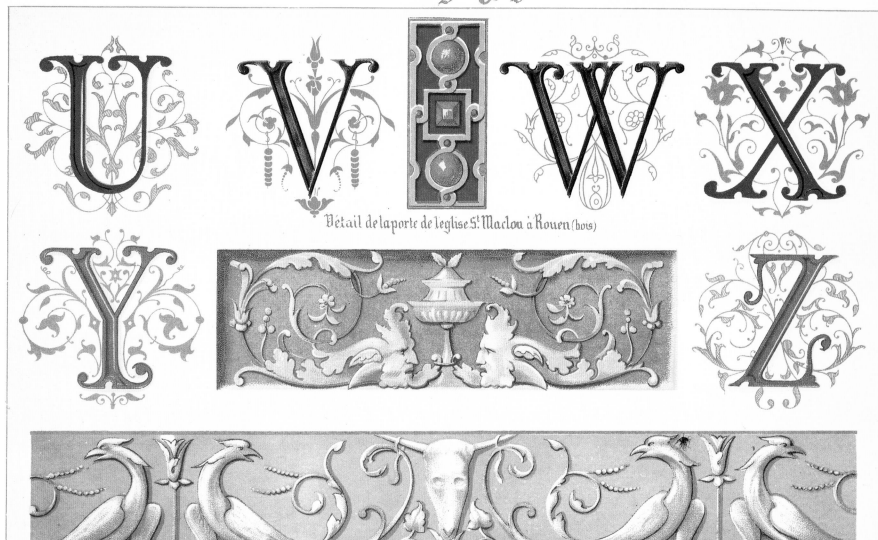

Détail de la porte de l'église St Maclou à Rouen (bois)

Frises tirées du Château de Blois.

INDEX